GUIDE FOR THE CHRISTIAN ASSEMBLY

THIERRY MAERTENS — JEAN FRISQUE

GUIDE FOR THE CHRISTIAN ASSEMBLY

REVISED EDITION

Feasts Superseding Sundays
Indexes to the New Lectionary
Calendar and Biography of Saints
General Indexes to the Guides

Fides/Claretian
Notre Dame, Indiana 46556

Translated from the French by MOLAISE MEEHAN, O.S.B.

Nihil Obstat: V. Descamps
can. libr. cens.

Imprimatur: J. Thomas, *vic. gen.*
Tournai, September 20, 1971

LCCCN: 72-114245

ISBN: 0-8190-0009-4

1773

Translated from the original French edition,
Guide de l'assemblée chrétienne, Casterman, 1970.
An edition of St. Andrews Abbey, Bruges.

CONTENTS

FIRST PART

FEASTS SUPERSEDING SUNDAYS

February 2nd

THE PRESENTATION OF JESUS

A. THE WORD

I. Malachi 3:1-4
1st reading

Malachi, or the author concealed behind that name, compiled his prophecies after the reconstruction of the temple was already completed (5th century B.C.). But, despite the legislation of Leviticus, the priestly caste is far from being reformed.

In fact what is required is the reform of the people as a whole, but the prophet concentrates on the temple and its cult. The malaise of the people affects the temple, and reciprocally, a degraded cult becomes a cause of decadence among the people. The interdependence is all the more acute because those responsible for Israel now are the religious leaders. Since the exile, she has lost her political autonomy.

a) Malachi resolutely places himself in the line of a *theocratic messianism* where the coming of Yahweh in person is contemplated, rather than a royal messiah. There was certainly no person at that time capable of kindling messianic hope. Thus he prefers to rely on Yahweh himself to whom he gives the titles "Lord" and "angel of the alliance." Yahweh however will be preceded by a precursor, a "messenger" (v. 1), who is somewhat mysterious and fulfills doubtless the function foreseen in Isaiah 40:3; 57:14.

b) The theocracy envisaged is a *cultic* one. Yahweh's coming will be the occasion of a profound renewal of the priestly caste. The "purification" which has been so long foreseen will apply especially to the Levites (v. 3) who will return to their ancestors' ideal of fidelity (v. 4; cf. Ex 32:26-29; Nb 25:7-13; Dt 33:8-11). Thus Malachi's messianic ideal approaches that of Ezechiel: a cultic theocracy strongly based on perfection of rite and a moral purification which is linked to progress in social justice (v. 5, not in our reading).

The choice of this lesson for the feast of the Lord's Presentation seemed mandatory. The third evangelist himself suggests it (see below) by referring to Malachi 3. It is Yahweh himself who comes in the person of the infant Jesus to purify the cult and save the people.

II. Hebrews 2:14-18
2nd reading

The author of Hebrews devotes the early portion of his letter (He 1-2) to a demonstration of the superiority in the order of salvation of the incarnate Son of God over the angels. This superiority Jesus owes to his humanity. In other words it is by virtue of his humanity that he is the true mediator of human salvation.

a) In verses 14-16 there is insistence on *consanguinity*—the same flesh and blood—as between the Son and the "great number of sons" (He 2:10) whom God wishes to lead to glory. Such sharing of the human condition, even unto death (v. 14), was necessary if the Son was to render powerless the Master of death, and deliver men (by his resurrection) from the slavery that weighed upon them (v. 15).

b) In verses 17-18 the author affirms that it is by virtue of this sharing in the human condition, to the point of trial by suffering, that Jesus exercises his *priestly* power of "merciful and faithful high priest" (v. 17), expiating for the people's sins. This idea will often recur later in the letter (cf. He 4:15; 5:8, etc.). Clearly the author's idea of Christ's priesthood is being diametrically opposed to Jewish and above all pagan nations. For the latter, the salva-

tion that comes from God is always exterior to man: prie
always thought of as implying separation and isolation.

It is only required that the mediator of the New Covena
presented in the temple in order that we come to know the
of cult that is pleasing to the Father. It is one of perfect obedie
to the Father through full participation in the human conditio
Henceforward the Temple is the Body of Christ.

III. Luke 2:22-40 *Gospel*

In this passage we have in order the account of Jesus' presentation in the temple (vv. 22-28), the canticle attributed to Simeon (vv. 29-32), the prophecies of Simeon and Anna (vv. 33-38), and finally a brief statement about Jesus' life at Nazareth (vv. 39-40). The references to the Old Testament are sufficiently numerous to give the whole account its structure (chiefly Ml 3 concerning the arrival of Yahweh in his temple, and Dn 9, the prophecy of seventy weeks before God's manifestation).

a) Mary goes to the temple to be purified there, in accordance with Scripture (Lv 12:2-8) and brings Jesus with her for ransom as the first-born (Ex 13:11-13; 22:28-29; Lv 5:7). The child's presentation in the temple had to be made forty days after his birth. This, added to the nine months of gestation and the six months which separated the conception of Jesus from the appearance of Gabriel in the temple, makes seventy weeks, the time foretold by Daniel 9:21-26 as the prelude to *God's coming* (cf. Lk 1:26-38).

The references to Malachi 3 in the account are numerous (compare Ml 3:1 with Lk 2:22, the "day" of Ml 3:2 with Lk 2:22; the "just" of Ml 3:18-20 with Lk 2:25; the light of Ml 3:19 with Lk 2:32; the "oblation" of Ml 3:3-4, 6-10 with Lk 2:22; the "nations" of Ml 3:12 with Lk 2:32). Luke had seen in Gabriel's apin the temple (Lk 1:11) the fulfillment of the sending of el in Malachi 3:1a. Now in the entry to the temple he sees parition of Yahweh that had been foretold in Malachi 3:1b. verses 29-32 he inserts Simeon's canticle to the "glory" of st (cf. Is 40:6; 60:1-3). In the Old Testament this glory resented Yahweh himself and brought about the death of nyone who gazed on it (Ex 19:21; 33-20; Gn 32:31; Dt 4:33; Wi 6:22-23). But now, in Jesus, Yahweh is residing among his people in such fashion as to be heard and seen.

b) Luke likewise insists on the redemptive and paschal role of Jesus. Though he is God, he is destined for humiliation and *death.*

We find this theme in the canticle attributed to Simeon, where glory and death are envisioned together (vv. 26, 30, 32). It is as if the divine presence among humanity can be discerned only in the mystery of death, as if the simple fact of seeing God were already leading man into the world of eschatology. It is the final verses above all of Simeon's prophecy (vv. 33-35) that closely associate Jesus' humiliation and suffering with his glory and his mission. By making him the "light of nations" (v. 32) Simeon is borrowing a theme from the theology of the suffering servant (Is 49:6). Luke follows this insight at the end of the passage by describing the lowliness of Jesus' family life (vv. 39-40).

The Messiah will bring division and contradiction (v. 34; cf. Is 8:12-15). Because of him a sword will pierce the soul of Mary (v. 35), in accordance with Ezechiel's prophecies (Ez 5:1; 6:3; 21:1-22 and especially 14:17) where the sword symbolizes the approaching punishment of a part of Israel. Mary is made to realize that her personal sorrow symbolizes that of the people as a whole (Lk 1:26-38). Her own pilgrimage of faith will impose ruptures that will associate her with the "transfixed Messiah" (Ze 12:10).

Christ will be a bright light for the nations, but at the same time a cause for crisis among a people, torn because of the nature of the proposed salvation and the character of the

Messiah himself. To the day of calvary Mary will have to endure this tension, a mother's sorrow at the death of her son, and the sorrow-laden pilgrimage of faith.

As he has elicited it from his scriptural sources, Luke provides the insight into the temple presentation, indicating the mystery of Christ in his being and his action. By closely associating Mary with this, he emphasizes for the disciples the way they must choose if they are to follow her example.

B. DOCTRINE

The Theme of the Temple

A fairly normal attitude of Christians is detachment where their places of worship are concerned, those stone churches where the Eucharist is celebrated. This does not necessarily indicate a distaste for religious practice: Christians simply feel that when they gather for Mass the place where they gather does not matter very much. It could be a church, the open air, or any place whatever, so far as some people are concerned.

For a few this reaction is even more pronounced and indicates a real change of attitude. It is not the practicing Christian they think who is the worthwhile one: the person who attends Mass daily is even looked upon with suspicion. For them the true Christian is the person who bears witness to the gospel in his daily life and exhibits a true love of his brothers.

On the other hand we have today non-practicing Christians or even indeed non-Christians, particularly in rural areas, who remain so attached to their churches that they oppose the suppression of any place of worship or any rearrangement of parishes. Even when there is practically no attendance they will not countenance the discontinuance of Mass in their village.

The feast of the Lord's presentation is a good opportunity for reflecting on these various attitudes and measuring their validity. Throughout salvation history the temple theme has seen considerable development. Biblical sources will enable us to see how the faith has progressively influenced the religious man's concept of genuine worship and the place where it is conducted.

The Jerusalem temple

Temples play a preponderant role in all religions. Placed in a profane world, man, as he seeks salvation, looks for ways of communicating with the divine. The various liturgical celebrations which punctuate his life offer him the best means of doing this. A liturgy however cannot be carried out in any and every place: it will be efficacious only when associated with some place that escapes the dimension of the secular and is mysteriously linked with divine energy. At such places, mountains, springs, etc., were erected sanctuaries where proper cult could be offered to divinities. Pagan man's natural concept of a temple indicates the nature of his religious quest. He looks for salvation in something stable and solid, something superior to the ravages of time.

It was not until the reign of Solomon that Israel had her temple on the mount of Sion, the capital of the kingdom. There was some opposition to this. Some feared that a temple of stone would assimilate the religion of the covenant to pagan religions. Prior to this Israel possessed a movable sanctuary only, around which the people gathered on great occasions. Solomon's temple was destroyed when Jerusalem was captured, but after the return from exile it was rebuilt and became the religious center of Judaism.

We cannot understand the proper meaning of the Jewish temple without taking account of the prophet's attitude. It is very clear that for them Yahweh is not necessarily linked with it. If the cult is too formalist he is absent from it. The cult he wishes is rooted in men's hearts. When the people are unfaithful to their God, one must look for the return of Yahweh in a new temple to the messianic future. The former cult will be rejected for the definitive cult of the final times. To this new temple of God even the nations will have access.

Meanwhile some important movements, such as the Essene, took a position hostile to the temple, its worship and its pilgrimages. In their fashion they were demonstrating how optional it really was.

The definitive temple, the body of Christ

In the life of Jesus of Nazareth the Jerusalem temple had an important place. A few weeks after his birth he was presented there by Mary, his mother. At the age of twelve we find him there among the doctors. Throughout his public life he regularly went on pilgrimages to pray there and to preach the Good News.

Thus Jesus fits into the living tradition of his people, following the pattern of the pious Jew for whom the Jerusalem temple is the focus of the most authentic piety (see the psalms). For all this however, he sets himself against everything that is opposed to genuine cult and sorts out what is pure from what is not. John has good reason for placing the episode of the expulsion of the sellers from the temple at the first visit to Jerusalem. Jesus could not enter the temple without making the gesture that restored it to its proper function. It is a house of prayer, not of commerce.

John goes further when he sees this initial gesture as a condemnation of the temple itself. The real temple of the new covenant is the body of Christ himself. The sign of this that Jesus will give is his own passion.

The truth is that, with the intervention of the man-God, a profound change has taken place. He is the only one capable of a worship that is pleasing to God, obedience of the heart that goes the length of death, the death of the cross. And so his body, in its passion, becomes the only temple where sacrifice worthy of the name is offered, the one visible reality that should be acknowledged as sacred. By his passion the Jerusalem temple becomes desacralized, and its transitory character becomes manifest. For all that it is the Mount of Sion, it is not a sacral spot. True worship is worship in spirit and in truth. Of this Christ alone is priest and victim. All particularism is at an end: in the dead and risen Jesus everyone has access to true worship, but only in him.

The Church, the body of Christ, temple of the Holy Spirit

Because she is the Body of Christ, the Church is the only temple here below of worship pleasing to God. There Jesus continues to offer the unique sacrifice of the new covenant. In all members of the Church the Spirit is working to elicit the filial cry "Father, thy will be done."

This temple of the new covenant is composed of living stones. "I exhort you then, brothers, by the mercy of God, to offer your persons as a living sacrifice, holy and pleasing to God. This is the spiritual worship you must render" (Rm 12:1).

There is no ecclesial institution comparable to the Jerusalem temple. That would be impossible. The Church is made up above all of her members, and this should never be forgotten. Too often the concept of the "Church" suggests an "institution," and the ecclesial mystery becomes distorted. It is hard perhaps to avoid the mistake. Even when proper emphasis is laid on persons there is a tendency to see them only as actually assembled by the Church. As if the Church had no existence independent of its assembled members. This sort of thinking is traceable to clergy and should be overcome, something indeed that recent conciliar works have been trying to accomplish. The Church is the people of God. She develops into an institution, but it is not merely an institution. Wherever her members are, she is, because she is above all her members. When she gathers these for the Eucharist she develops an institutional character. But when they are not gathered but dispersed among men, she must still exist as the leaven in the mass. She must be the light of the world and provide for men the sign of that salvation which is acquired once for all in Jesus Christ.

Once all this is remembered, it is true that the Church's mission leads her to build churches of stone. Genuine worship must have a liturgical dimension. Such buildings however will always be designed to fulfill the requirements of the spiritual cult that is accessible to all.

Mission, the sign of the temple and churches of stone

For some years it has been customary to stress the ecclesial dimension of all evangelism by describing the object of mission as the "implanting of the Church." The suggestion of the phrase for those who used it was the foundation of a local church with the whole network of auxiliary institutions that would ensure its normal functioning. The remark would be added that "mission does not consist in converting souls."

Some reaction indeed was necessary against an overly individualist concept of mission but it leaned unduly toward the institutional. The implanting of the Church means that the mystery of Christ must be engrafted into a people's spiritual itinerary. Between Christ present in his envoys and the people in question, must take place the dramatic dialogue of faith.

The missionary, who is a man of the Church, must, in imitation of Christ, make the "sign of the temple" to appear. Like Christ, he knows that he has come to destroy among the people he evangelizes all religious particularism. He must make prophetic gestures similar to that by which Jesus chased the sellers from the temple. The purpose of a temple is prayer to the Father, and this will imply a deep-rooted adjustment on the part of the missionary to the spiritual quest of the people he evangelizes. To the question which will be asked "What sign do you give for acting thus?" he can give no other reply but that of Jesus. The sign is Jesus' passion, prolonged in those whom he sends. The sign of the temple of the new covenant is the configuration of the Church to Christ's death. Under such circumstances true worship can take place, worship that is pleasing to God and open to all. It is a cult of obedience unto the death of the cross, a cult of love without limits, which implies total self-renunciation.

If the spirit which animates the missionary is truly a spirit of

Catholicity, rooted in the most authentic sources, his acculturation will be well under way. Churches will be built of stone, institutions will develop, but the tendency simply to export what one has known at home will always be guarded against.

The eucharistic sign of the spiritual temple

When the Church assembles the faithful for the Eucharist, she is inviting them to enter deeper and deeper into the sacrifice of Christ, and to offer their persons in him as a sacrifice agreeable to God. Thus she builds herself as a spiritual temple. In her assemblies however she is guided by a realization of what man is in actuality, body and soul. If spiritual cult be a cult of love without limits this should be evident in the assembly itself. Thus every ecclesial assembly should exhibit the note of catholicity. Diversity is altogether natural at the Eucharist, because in Jesus Christ all are already brothers. The brotherhood that has been already realized in Christ must penetrate the whole being of Christians, and the Church should ensure that her assemblies are not purely replicas of natural communities. The eucharistic sign of the spiritual temple will be evident to the extent that the place of celebration is open to Christians of every race and every social level. So many of our places of worship do not answer this description, and means must be found of changing them. The issue at stake is a grave one: the note, that is, of Catholicism in the Church, which must be made evident in Christian assembly.

March 19

SAINT JOSEPH, SPOUSE OF THE VIRGIN MARY

A. THE WORD

I. 2 Samuel 7:4-5a, 12-14a, 16 *1st reading*	This reading, an extract from Nathan's prophecy (2 S 7:4-16), is well constructed and contains all the important points. For their proper understanding however they have to be set in their proper context.

a) As delivered, the prophecy of Nathan was designed to allay David's misgivings concerning the *future of his dynasty and his people.* The nation he ruled was not homogenous, as is clear from the successive anointings in the South (2 S 2:1-4), the North (2 S 5:1-3) and at Jerusalem (2 S 5:6-10). He wondered whether after his death the kingship would endure. Nathan replies to this question. As he had done for David, God will protect his successor and assure his kingship (v. 12). Saul's failure will not necessarily affect the future of the davidic kingdom.

b) The predictions of Nathan, a court prophet, constitute a contemporary message only. It was subsequent reflection that gave them *messianic* import, beginning with the author's incorporation of them in his book. Verses 14 and 15 have a deuteronomic flavor, and guarantee the perpetuity of the davidic dynasty, provided at least that its members conduct themselves properly. Verse 16 likewise affirms the establishment "for always" of the dynasty. Understood thus, the prophecy was destined to have an unprecedented future. It becomes the source of all royal messianism, and the text is subjected to several rereadings that intensify its message (1 Ch 17; Pss 131/132:11-12 and 88/89:30-38).

c) A very important theme is that of the *house*. To establish his dynasty and provide a center for his people, David had contemplated the erection of a house to shelter the ark of the covenant (2 S 7:1-3). Through his prophet, Yahweh conveys to him that he himself will build a house for the king (vv. 11b and 16). This does not mean that God is refusing the temple—it will be built by Solomon, as verse 13, doubtless a later addition, indicates. But the future of the people and the dynasty should depend rather on the covenant between Yahweh and his kings than on the temple itself. Mutual fidelity on God's part, and the king's, will prove more decisive for the history of the people than temple sacrifices. Subsequent tradition, Christian tradition above all, will follow this view and reject the temple (Is 66:1-2; Ac 7:48; Lk 23:44-45; Jn 2:19).

In the person of Jesus of Nazareth Nathan's prophecy finds its fulfillment. Joseph's role is to assure the line of descent: he is of David's house. In Jesus it becomes clear what house God wishes to construct for humanity: the house is his very body (cf. Jn 2:21). In him is established the definitive covenant between God and man. There being no longer reason for the temple of stone, it can disappear.

II. Romans 4:13, 16-18, 22
2nd reading

This reading is taken from Paul's analysis of the relations between faith and justification, following the precedent of Abraham (Rm 4). We are given two principal points of the argument.

a) Why is it that faith, not works, brings justification? Paul replies that faith corresponds to God's way with man. Were he to come to man with a contract, works would then certainly be the most adequate human response. But he comes with a *promise*, a gratuitous gift, that is, wherein he retains the initiative (vv. 13 and 16). The works of the law are useless if one endeavors by means of them to gain the object of the promise: an heir does not endeavor to seize control of the heritage.

b) The other argument is barely sketched (vv. 17-18). The promise was made to Abraham before he was yet circumcised. But God envisaged for him a *universal paternity* (Gn 17:5). Thus it is contrary to God's will to limit Abraham's posterity to the circumcised. Every believer has Abraham as father. God has the power to make the dead themselves beneficiaries of the promise.

The portrait of Joseph presented by the gospel is that of the model believer altogether open to God's will. God's manifestation to him is however disconcerting. He is the man who has "hoped against all hope." He is a true descendant of Abraham, his religion being that of the Promise.

III. Matthew 1:16, 18-21, 24a *Alternative Gospel*

In this gospel we have two fragments, the first confined to a single verse (1:16) which concludes the "genealogy" of Jesus, as constructed by Matthew to emphasize the davidic ancestry of the Messiah; the second (1:18-21) being the "Annunciation to Joseph." The literary genre represented by the latter should be properly understood. These annunciations of birth in the Bible follow a particular pattern. In each case we have the apparition of an angel. The person concerned is addressed by a name which recalls his function (here *Joseph, son of David*, a title given him by the angel on this occasion only). An obstacle has to be surmounted (usually the woman's sterility; here, for Joseph, the fact that she is a virgin). A sign is given as guarantee (here, the marvelous birth), and finally there are precisions about the naming of the child (here, Jesus). The literary genre is simply a manner of describing a real event with ancedotal details.

A comparison between this annunciation and that to Mary (Lk 1:26-38) will enable us to see the nuances peculiar to Matthew. All of these combine to give us insight into the religious personality of Joseph.

At the annunciation the angel had told Mary that her son would be a son of David (Lk 1:32) and had then spoken of the conception (Lk 1:34-35). With Joseph the procedure is different. The conception is an accomplished fact (Mt 1:30), and he is reassured about the *davidic sonship* of the child (vv. 20-21).

Mary had been disturbed about the question of her bethrothal: Joseph is disturbed about his role where the child is concerned.

Mary had understood that she would give birth through the power of the Spirit, but the evangelists do not say that she told her husband. It is however probable that she did. Thus he is not disturbed about the virtue of his betrothed, and the angel does not appear to reassure him about this. He is, as the evangelist says, a "just" man (v. 19), not in terms of the legalist justice that would authorize repudiation of his betrothed, but with a religious justice which will not allow him to appropriate credit for God's action in the life and calling of his son. The angel's intervention is to show him that God has need of him. What Mary has conceived is of the Holy Spirit, but Joseph will have to introduce the child to the line of David and give him a name.

Joseph is a true believer. He fully respects God's work and tries to see more clearly the role proposed for himself. There is no trace of mere resignation in the picture Matthew presents. God will not save man without his cooperation and fidelity.

IV. Luke 2:41-51a *Alternative Gospel*

The episode recounted in today's gospel, Jesus among the doctors, is not to be regarded as in any way unusual. Set in the general context of the third gospel, the first ascent to Jerusalem is a sort of prophecy of the final one at the Pasch. The reaction of his parents is of a piece with that of believers searching for their Lord, with all the bafflement that this quest entails.

a) Luke certainly sees the event in the light of the *death and resurrection of Jesus.* Of the parents of Jesus he says that "they did not understand" (v. 50). In the third gospel this phrase is applied to the disciples each time they failed to understand the significance of Jesus' proclamations concerning his ascent to Jerusalem (Lk 9:43-45; 18:34; 24:25-26) to encounter there his passion and death.

The reproach addressed by Jesus to his parents *"Did you not know that I must . . ."* (v. 49) is so formulated by Luke in order to direct attention to the Scriptures as understood by Jesus, particularly to those oracles concerned with his death and resurrection (Lk 9:22; 13:33; 17:25; 22:37; 24:7 and above all 24:27; 24:44). It is tantamount to saying "Have you not read this in the Scriptures? Is not the realization of these prophecies inevitable?"

Nor are parallels of detail lacking between this first ascent to Jerusalem and that which will bring him to the cross. In both cases we have the search for Jesus (vv. 44-45; cf. Lk 24:3, 23-24) for three days (v. 47; cf. Lk 24:7, 21, 46). In both it is the Father's will which determines Jesus' behavior (v. 49; cf. Lk 22:42). In both cases the episode occurs during the Pasch (v. 41; cf. Lk 22:1).

b) The verb "seek" which is repeated four times in the account (vv. 44, 45, 48, 49) belongs to the biblical theme of *search for God*. God is not, like the idols, someone who lets himself be easily found. The search was first undertaken by the nomad patriarchs who found in history the fulfillment of God's plan. Subsequently, after a more spiritual fashion, we have the search for God in the law (Ps 118/119). Later still, above all in the exile, the people set themselves to find God in obedience to his will (Dt 4:29; Is 55:6; Jr 29:13-14; Ps 104/105:1-4—in most of these texts note the "seek-find" association).

With Christ the search for God becomes the "search for the Lord." He cannot be found in the human environment of the family (v. 44) but "in the Father's house" (v. 49). Blinded by legalism, the Jews seek him but cannot find him (Jn 7:34; 8:21). Only charity (Jn 13:33-34), prayer (Mt 7:7-8) and faith (Jn 20:11-15; Lk 24:5) can attain the object of the search.

As given us by Luke, the episode of Jesus among the doctors clarifies considerably for us important aspects of the pilgrimage of faith. Joseph and Mary are authentic believers. Faith however does not arise spontaneously: one must be content at first not to understand the wisdom of God. The true believer will go in search of God, an indefinite quest that will continually call for self-renunciation. God lets himself be found by those who, while searching, discern in the distance their Lord's cross.

B. DOCTRINE

The Theme of the Promise

Christians are generally aware that faith cannot be reduced to religious practice, that it must be translated into daily life in a behavior of which the gospel gives us the essential norms. It is however noteworthy that faith, as generally practiced, falls far short of the rich horizons indicated by the Bible. Faith is a dynamism capable of marshaling a man's most secret energies for a spiritual adventure that will engage him totally. But it is too often understood as merely something which requires conformity to a set of moral principles. Biblical faith on the other hand uses the language of love. It begets a deep personal relationship; it sets up reciprocal fidelity.

Faith in the promises is one of the special themes of both Old and New Testaments. This rather than anything else reveals the original character of the process of faith. We find it throughout all stages of Israel's history: Yahweh is the god of the promises. It would however require the coming of Christ to give the theme its definitive shape. Human salvation is accomplished at the moment when the man-God himself makes a promise. And what he promises is the Spirit. Now is established the order of love between God and humanity.

The feast of Saint Joseph invites us to reflect on the theme of the promise. This best reveals to us his spiritual personality as presented by the New Testament. And in this sense we are all concerned in the celebration.

Yahweh, God of the promises

The language of promise is in fact foreign to man's natural tendency, in his search for salvation. This arises from his deep need for security. Salvation is seen as divinization, and men will try to develop a spiritual way that will automatically bring about communion with the sacral world, which is essentially stable and immutable. The gods do not intervene, and consequently do not make promises. The order of persons and things has been permanently established in a definitive way. Nothing can happen. Man's only problem is the finding of adequate means to integrate himself in this.

Israel's spiritual quest, the pilgrimage of faith, was otherwise. Jewish realism *vis-a-vis* the event made this people realize gradually that salvation did not lie within their own resources. It depended on the altogether gratuitous initiative of God. Him they recognized as the Totally-Other God, the only one who controlled the salvation men sought. Recognized, in the event, he was seen as the living God, the God who intervenes, the God who reveals himself. God as seen by faith is essentially personal. If he intervenes in Israel's history, this is to set up a personal relationship with the people he has chosen.

Thus, it is easy to see how, for Israel, he becomes the God of promises. Whoever has encountered the living God and based himself on his power and fidelity, very quickly senses that our salvation belongs to the order of promise, to the most delicate domain, that is, of the order of love. When Yahweh promises, he binds himself, as only God can bind, with the bonds of love. He discovers that the fulfillment sought by man can only come at the end of a long history. It requires time for the reciprocal relations of love to take root. As is to be expected in a love relationship, the fulfillment is not foreseeable.

It is clear that Israel questioned herself about the content of

God's promises, and her reflections in this matter developed as her faith deepened. At the beginning it was favors and blessings that were sought from God: a fruitful territory, numerous posterity, power among nations, all tangible blessings. But in the end it is God himself who is the object of the promise, his favor and his grace, because God is sufficient. At this point the meaning of the promise becomes clear: it belongs to the order of love.

Jesus Christ, the yes of God's promises

To affirm that Jesus of Nazareth fulfills God's promises is to encounter the essential mystery of Jesus Christ and discover the essential meaning of the order of promise. Jesus is the man-God, the greatest gift God makes of himself to humanity, because of love. But simultaneously he is the one man among men who actively and perfectly responds to the antecedent initiative of God. This he does because of the double love for God and all men. He saves man because, in his person, the definitive encounter between God and man takes place.

The order of promise is seen to be one of communion between persons. God's promise is the gift of himself in his incarnate Son. It does not offer any easy security, or any possession other than the fullness of this gift which is sufficient of itself. One cannot merit such a gift, or gain it by the observance of any law. It is altogether gratuitous, open to all who accept it. The reservations of the Old Testament are completely overcome. Reread in the light of Christ, the whole pilgrimage of Israel, as Saint Paul well knew, is seen to be dominated by manifestations of the God of the promise. Reciprocity is accomplished in Christ, because the incarnate Word is the one man among men who can tender to God the yes of a perfect fidelity, answering to God's own fidelity. God always retains the sovereign initiative in the order of promise, but man's active response is none the less an essential element. Without man, God will not save man. Such is the fundamental law of the religion of love.

But the order of promise goes further still. With its accomplishment in Jesus Christ, because of the law of love, comes as it were a new departure. Throughout his public life Jesus himself continued to make promises. Saint John, who sees the fundamental always, focuses all of these in the single promise of the Spirit. In the Spirit would be consummated the order of love between God and man. The promise is doubly significant. On the one hand the salvation of all mankind depends altogether on Jesus Christ. On the other, Jesus only inaugurated salvation. It becomes an ongoing history where each person is called upon to respond personally to God's initiative.

The promise an ecclesial heritage

The Church holds the promise as an inheritance. She has her beginnings in the sending of the Spirit, who fulfills the double promise of the Father and the incarnate Word. The descent of the Spirit on the apostles is evidence that the Risen Lord is really present in his Church, and that the Church is really the Body of Christ. The Spirit comes to all those who through baptism receive the gift of filial adoption and are conformed to the only-begotten Son.

What is the meaning of this coming of the Spirit upon all members of the Body? It defines the essential state of the Christian, who is heir to the promise. He is a man possessed by the Trinitarian God. In Jesus Christ, God gives himself personally to his adoptive son. The Christian in turn, through his link with Christ, finds the power to respond actively to God's initiative of love. If he has received the Spirit, it is the proof that he too can utter that filial yes which is pleasing to the Father. All Christians are introduced to a dialogue of real reciprocity with God, as the order of love requires.

Why then does the New Testament affirm that here below Christians inherit merely the earnest of the promise? The reason is to emphasize that the gift of the Spirit reaches plenitude only after death: on earth the history of the promise continues to unfold. When the Christian receives the Holy Spirit in baptism and confirmation he finds himself confronted by a task, that of bringing his particular stone for the building of the Kingdom. Gradually, as he makes his pilgrimage in obedience and love, his faith takes definite shape. Sharing the promise is not the mere reception of a gift, but above all the assumption of new responsibility. The period of waiting for definitive fulfillment of the promise is not without meaning: on this earth is gradually built up the Kingdom of God.

Those for whom the promise is destined comprise Gentiles as well as Jews: it is destined for all men. It is addressed exclusively to faith: the bonds set up by the Spirit between God and men are inevitably those of communion in love, and God gives himself only to the man who welcomes him in poverty. In the order of promise all privilege is abolished. The reason why no one can establish a right where it is concerned, is because it is genuinely proffered to all.

History of the promise and its realization in mission

The sending of the Holy Spirit to the Church makes her aware of her missionary dynamism. It is this sending which identifies her as the Body of Christ, the temple of dialogue between God and humanity: and it continues to be an active process until the day when the Church will attain her true stature. It is not something which took place once for all on the first Pentecost day.

Mission is simply the translation into act of the sending of the Spirit. Its objective is growth in the Church, and wherever the Church is implanted, the Spirit is sent. The Church receives this gift in order simply that she send the Spirit in turn, after the example of Christ. It is essential that this be affirmed, if we are to understand the meaning of ecclesial anointing in the Spirit in configuration with Christ the Head. Such is the Christian's dignity. He is aware of his missionary responsibility, a sharer in the promise, cooperating as a member of the ecclesial Body in the constant sending of the Spirit by Christ. The Church's mission is fully comprehensible only in reference to the very mystery of the Trinity.

But it does not follow, because mission is linked to the sending of the Spirit, that the Spirit's action is limited to the frontiers of the Church. From the day of creation, God's Spirit has filled the whole universe. God's grace is at work in every man and among every people, leading them secretly to the encounter with Jesus Christ in his Body which is the Church. It accompanies every spiritual quest. Yet, wherever the Church has not yet touched men in the course of her mission, the Spirit is not yet sent. A sending of the Spirit always implies that here the grace of God is flowering in a Church. A new people is entering the temple of encounter with the living God.

When we understand the manner in which mission is linked with the sending of the Spirit, we understand too the nature of missionary witness. One cannot really be a missionary without having encountered oneself the living God of Jesus Christ, without being personally caught up in the reciprocal bonds of love. Missionary witness is the supreme expression of a faith that has found in Jesus Christ the reason for the self-renunciation that is necessary. Love is the only key.

The sending of the Spirit on the eucharistic community

On Pentecost Day the Holy Spirit came down on the assembled apostles; and, immediately afterwards, they bore witness to the Risen Christ who was present among them. Every eucharistic celebration is a new Pentecost: it is, in the Church, the place *par excellence* of descent by the Spirit, of sharing in the promise. Here the Risen Christ is most genuinely present with his own.

The members who attend are constantly being drawn into deeper encounter with the God of Jesus Christ. Bound by a living bond to the Risen Lord, they sing God's praises, give thanks for his marvelous initiative of salvation, and know that they have access to the Father because in Jesus Christ they are adoptive sons. When, all together, they pray the Our Father, it is the Spirit that is at work in them. After Mass, they return to daily life amid their brothers, with the renewed conviction that they have but one really important task. They must bear witness to what they have become under the Spirit's action, and participate in the Church's missionary dynamism, so that the history of the promise may continue to unfold.

March 25

THE ANNUNCIATION

A. THE WORD

I. Isaiah 7:10-14 *1st reading*

Under the reign of Achaz (713-716) the kings of Aram and of Israel joined forces to place a king friendly to them at Jerusalem who would not be of the davidic line (Is 7:1, 6; cf. 2 K 16:5-9). Isaiah goes to meet Achaz (in 735?) to calm his fears. The davidic dynasty will be maintained, if the king keeps his faith in Yahweh's promises untarnished (Is 7:9b). The prophet however doubtless fears that he will fail, because he is accompanied by his son whose name means "a remnant shall return" (Is 7:3).

a) By refusing all signs from heaven Achaz ranges himself among the unbelievers. At verse 11 Yahweh is still the God of Achaz ("your" God): at verse 13 he is the God of Isaiah only ("my" God) and of those who believe. Unlike Achaz, the Emmanuel will choose the good and reject the evil (Is 7:15).

The Emmanuel is put forward as a sign, the sign of God's fidelity which is the basis of *faith*. This faith it is which will establish the "Remnant" of the believers and guarantee their deliverance. We encounter one of the principal axes in Isaian prophecy: the new people will be qualitative, the product of faith not of any national privileges (cf. Is 28:16-17).

b) Who are Emmanuel and his mother? It is not stated that the "girl" (v. 14) will give birth in *virginity*. The word *halmah* could belong to the vocabulary of court literature and designate a woman of the royal dynasty or a queen. In order to identify the Emmanuel we must remember the historical context. What Isaiah has in mind above all is the birth of a child of royal blood (doubtless Ezechias, as in Is 11:1-8). However the prophet's horizons are not limited by this: his messianic hope is at once immediate and far-reaching. The coming Messiah is incarnate in a concrete person; but his characteristics remain mysterious. In other words the expected salvation is at hand. It can come at any moment, though its time of coming transcends all calculation and is a divine secret. At a later stage a gradually increasing stress will be laid on eschatology in messianic hope. In the Septuagint the girl who is to bear the child will be described as a virgin. That is the version used in Matthew 1:22-23 to affirm that the prophecy of Isaiah has found fulfillment in the birth of Jesus from Mary.

II. Hebrews 10:4-10
2nd reading

In chapters 7-9 the author of the letter to the Hebrews has established in detail the superiority of Christ's sacrifice to those of the old covenant. Our reading here is taken from a recapitulatory chapter (He 10:1-18), the whole economy of temple sacrifices being analyzed by contrast with that of Christ.

a) To understand the passage we should remember the biblical theme of the *sacrifice of the poor* (cf. Dn 3:38-40). Trial and exile had put an end to the quantitative sacrifices of the old temple, and had substituted the sacrifice of the poor. This corresponded to the misery of the times, and it had the dimensions of thanksgiving, repentance and humility. No longer is God to be reached by bloody sacrifices, but by obedience and love. Among the psalms which echo this doctrine, 39/40 is one of the most important (it is the meditation psalm for this feast). It hymns the discovery by a sick man that God does not expect sacrifices from him, but obedience and total fidelity to his law. From now on, for the sick man, moral behavior will constitute the essence of cult. By placing the psalm on the lips of Christ (vv. 5-7) the author is seeking to define the true nature of the sacrifice of the cross. It is not any more the immolation of a victim, however choice, but the expression of Christ's communion with his Father (vv. 7 and 9).

b) It is important that we know exactly what the *Father's will* was concerning Christ, and what obedience Jesus rendered in return. At no time was the Father's will the death of his Son. Such would be the attitude of a sanguinary God, who could only be appeased by the blood of someone dear to him. We should understand God's plan as one of having his Son share the human condition with sufficient love to transfigure it. Death of course is part of the human condition.

In order to describe the Father's will, our author makes use of some variants in Psalm 39/40 ("fashioned a body" v. 5), and at the moment of incarnation puts the sentiment on Christ's lips ("in entering the world" v. 5). In so doing he refers the sacrificial intention of Christ to the antecedent trinitarian state. This indicates the deep source of Christ's obedience: his whole human life can be said to have a sacrificial dimension. The cross does no more than seal it.

The reading that has been chosen for the Annunciation leads us to an understanding of the life of Mary, one patterned on and in continuity with the spiritual sacrifice of Christ. His initial "yes" had a sacrificial dimension which is revealed to us by the cross.

III. Luke 1:26-38 *Gospel*

This account is of a particular literary *genre*, a sort of midrash, where each word and phrase is loaded with association. To identify the essential thrusts we shall require a verse by verse commentary.

a) The historical background and context (vv. 26-27)

The appearance of the angel Gabriel places the annunciation scene in a prophetic and eschatological context. He was regarded by tradition as the depository of the secret of the seventy weeks, until the establishment of the definitive Kingdom (cf. Dn 8:16; 9:21; 24-26).

In fact Gabriel appeared first to Zachary in the temple (Lk 1:11), then to Mary six months later, 180 days, that is (Lk 1:26). Then after nine months (270 days) Christ appears in the world, and after forty days is presented in the temple. This makes 490 days in all, or seventy weeks, the stages of which are indicated by the phrase "when the days were accomplished" (Lk 1:23; 2:6, 22), giving the events the nature of prophecy-fulfillments.

Accordingly Christ is certainly the Messiah foreseen in Daniel 9, at once a human Messiah and the quasi-divine Son of Man (Dn 7:13). The events which proclaim his birth prepare for the entry into the definitive temple of Yahweh's glory, which is personified in Jesus.

b) The Titles of Mary (vv. 27-28)

The simplicity of this annunciation in a modest house in Galilee, a territory that was looked down on (Jn 1:46; 7:41), contrasts with the solemnity of the announcement of the Baptist's birth in the temple (Lk 1:5-25). Already we notice an opposition between Mary and Jerusalem. It is indicated in the angel's greeting, one which Zephaniah 3:16 and Zachary 9:9 address to Jerusalem, to tell her of the proximate coming of the Lord "in her womb" (the literal meaning of the formula in Ze 3:16). The angel is really transferring to Mary the privileges hitherto given to Jerusalem. The influence of Zephaniah indeed is pervasive throughout the account (Lk 1:28 and Ze 3:15; Lk 1:30 and Ze 3:16; Lk 1:28 and Ze 3:14).

For Saint Luke the phrase "full of grace" doubtless means that Mary was "comely," like Ruth before Booz (Rt 2:2, 10, 13), Esther before Assuerus (Est 2:9, 15, 17; 5:2, 8; 7:3; 8:5) or any woman in the eyes of her husband (Pr 5:19; 7:5; 18:22; Ct 8:10). This marriage imagery is very evocative. God has long been seeking a faithful spouse. He has rejected Israel, his former spouse (Ho

1-3) but is disposed to be "betrothed" once more. That Mary is addressed with a phrase common between spouses is an indication that in her God will accomplish the espousal promise of the Old Testament. In the person of Jesus the two natures, divine and human, will be united.

c) The Titles of the Messiah (vv. 31-33)

The first titles accorded to Jesus are inspired by the royal phraseology of Nathan's promises (2 S 7:11). Jesus will be "great" (cf. 2 S 7:11), Son of the Most High, a title reserved for great personages (Pss 2:7; 28/29:1; 81/82:6; 88/89:7) and the Messiah in 2 Samuel 7:14. He will sit on the throne of David (2 S 7:16; Is 9:6). The angel transcends Nathan's vision however when he predicts the extension of Jesus' reign to the house of Jacob (the the extension of Jesus' reign to the house of Jacob (the ten tribes of the North). He will bring about unity between Judah and Israel (Ez 37:15-28; Dn 7:14; Mi 5:4-7), while awaiting the opportunity to achieve unity between Israel and the nations.

The omission of the title Emmanuel for Mary's son (Is 7:14) is not surprising. Half a score of names were in fact envisaged for the Messiah; but no tradition had fixed upon "Jesus," which means "Yahweh our savior." This name suggests two Old Testament personages who played an important role in the history of the people: the judge Joshua in the desert (Si 46:1-2) and the priest Joshua at the return from exile (Ze 3:1-10; Ag 2:1-9). By encountering suffering and death, Jesus in turn will earn the title "savior" of humanity.

d) The circumstances of conception (vv. 34-38)

The angel foretells the conception of the child in terms borrowed from Exodus 40:35, where the appearance of the cloud indicates God's presence. The child about to be born will be the fruit of God's special intervention. He will belong to the same celestial, divine world that the cloud usually symbolizes (v. 35).

Such a divine intervention however presupposes a free partner

(v. 37). She had intended apparently to remain a virgin. Young girls could receive this permission from their husbands, in Essene circles especially. Nevertheless Mary's assertion about not knowing man (she did know Joseph) must be taken in the same symbolic sense as the whole midrash. She stands for Jerusalem, the object of the promise of fecundity. Not to know man, for Jerusalem, means living the misery of rejection and abandonment (cf. Is 60:15; 62:1-4). Mary takes upon herself the desolation of the rejected city, and purports to say that a new espousal will be celebrated in which God, in her person, will take back his former spouse. In the annunciation is accomplished the mystery of God's betrothal to his people. When Luke speaks of Mary and her virginity, it is in the precise context of her nuptial communion with God, with a view to fuller description of the fruit of that union, the Messiah. And belief in the virginity of Mary as the spiritual spouse of God amounts to an affirmation concerning Jesus himself. The basic point remains a christological one.

B. DOCTRINE

The theme discussed for the feast of the Immaculate Conception, "Mary and the history of salvation" (pp. 91-97) treats of Mary's *fiat* and her motherhood.

June 22

BIRTH OF SAINT JOHN THE BAPTIST

A. THE WORD

I. Jeremiah 1:4-10
1st reading Vigil

In a poem of three strophes Jeremiah describes his vocation.

a) The first strophe (vv. 4-5) stresses his *predestination.* This is manifested at three levels: preexistence in the divine mind, consecration in his mother's womb, and official investiture as prophet for the nations. This image of antecedence in time is a way of affirming total communion between God and his prophet.

b) Human speech is altogether incapable of carrying the word of God. For better realization of this truth Jeremiah has some difficulty in expressing himself (vv. 6-7). This is a common motif in prophetic vocations. Moses stammered (Ex 4:10-12). Isaiah had to purify his lips (Is 6:1-6). The greatest heralds of salvation were frequently victims of dumbness or stammering (Mk 7:31-37). This emphasizes the union between God and his prophet, and the relation between divine initiative and prophetic ministry. It also shows that the messianic times, when the word (the means of communication that is) will be given abundantly to everyone (Lk 1:65; 2:17, 38; Jl 3:1-2; Ac 2:1-3) are about to be unaugurated.

c) The last strophe stresses the courage necessary for a prophet (vv. 8-10). At the time of writing Jeremiah could already have experienced the people's hostility towards him. He compares himself to a soldier facing the enemy, or an upright judge who gives sentence impartially.

The account of Jeremiah's vocation is a good introduction to an understanding of the Baptist's religious personality. He too responds to a call of God which touched him in his mother's womb. He too will proclaim a word that is not his own, the imminence of a kingdom which, as defined by Jesus, will astonish even the Baptist himself. He too will experience the opposition of the people. He will be cast in prison and will die there.

II. 1 Peter 1:8-12
2nd reading Vigil

This reading is taken from the great doxology (1 P 1:3-12) which begins the first letter of Peter. It seems that the author is inspired by a primitive Christian hymn that may have been arranged in three successive strophes, devoted first to the praise of the Father, the author of the new creation (paraphrased in vv. 3-5), second to the Son, the object of our love throughout trial (vv. 6-9), finally to the Holy Spirit, who is at work among prophets and preachers (vv. 10-12). In Titus 3:4-8 we have another paraphrase of this hymn.

The passage chosen for the liturgy stresses some essential points in salvation history. We are reminded that Christ is at the center, and that it is in this context that the role of *prophets* and *evangelists* must be understood.

Such is the classical presentation in the earliest Christian preaching (cf. Peter's discourses in the Acts). It is shown how the prophets, as serious and reflective men, interpreted events and the laws of nature to proclaim the hope of an era when everything would have meaning in Christ (v. 11). In this quest, the end of which they could not see, the prophets have been authentic ministers of salvation history (v. 12). The profession they inaugurated is today filled by the preachers of the gospel (designated in v. 12 by the name "angels" or envoys, as in Lk 7:24, 9:52; Mt 24:31; Ga 4:14). These too examine events with the same insight and in the same Spirit. They find salvation at work there.

As presented by the New Testament, the Baptist's message throws into clear relief the bond between prophecy and the person of Christ. The Baptist is the precursor of the Messiah: he only intervenes to prepare the way of the Lord. All his career is shaped by the imminence of salvation in the person of Jesus. Deprived of this dimension, his prophecies would be bereft of meaning.

III. Luke 1:5-17
Gospel Vigil

For a considerable time it was believed that the account of the Baptist's infancy in Luke reproduced an earlier original which emanated from the Baptist's disciples. Today this view is discarded. The evangelist himself composed the account in a style deliberately reminiscent of the Septuagint. He did so at a time subsequent to the redaction of the gospel, when he was already contemplating the composition of the Acts. This explains the numerous literary and theological resemblances between Luke 1-2 and Acts 1-12, as well as the presentation of the Baptist as a precursor of apostolic kerygma (Lk 1:76-80).

a) The advanced age of Zachary and Elizabeth, and the latter's barrenness (v. 7) suggest to the author a comparison with Abraham and Sara (cf. vv. 7-8 with Gn 18:11; v. 13 with Gn 17:19; and v. 18 with Gn 15:8). The resemblance however is confined to this: we cannot conclude that Zachary is a new Abraham or the Baptist a new Isaac.

John the Baptist is put forward as a child of the tribe of Abia (v. 5), a fairly despised tribe if one is to judge from the adverse comments in the Talmud. Perhaps this explains the later break by John with the aristocratic, political priesthood in Jerusalem.

His birth is foretold as that of a *prophet*. All the characteristic traits are there: asceticism (v. 15; cf. Nb 6:1-8; Mt 11:18), vocation from birth (v. 15b; cf. Jeremiah in Jr. 1:5, the servant in Is 49:1-5 and Samuel in 1 S 1:11), possession of the Spirit (Jl 3:1-3) associating him in remarkable fashion with the apostles at Pentecost (Ac 4:8; 8:29; 6:3-5; 7:55). For Luke however it is the figure of Samuel above all who typifies the Baptist. Like Samuel (1 S 2:21) he is "great" in the presence of the Lord (v. 15), and he is born from a sterile womb (v. 15; cf. 2 S 1:11). Just as Samuel was priest and prophet at once, entrusted with choice of the king, so is the Baptist, commissioned to point out the Messiah (Lk 3:21-22; 1 S 16:12-13).

The final characteristic trait is that John is to be, like Elias, a precursor. To indicate this Luke cites Malachi 3:23-24 as corrected by Sirach 48:10-11.

b) The *messenger angel.* The angel Gabriel, whose role for Luke is messianic (cf. Dn 8:16; 9:21), appears during the course of a liturgy (v. 11). Because sacrifice was the occasion *par excellence* of encounter between God and his people, it is normal that angels commissioned to transmit to men the divine will should appear in the smoke of sacrifice (Gn 22:11-18; Jg 6:20-22; 13:16-20; 1 Ch 21:18-30; Gn 28:12). Probably Luke is influenced by the traditional Jewish accounts of the birth of high priests such as John Hyrcanus or Ismael. He also sees in the angel's apparition (Lk 1-2, *passim;* Ac 1:10; 5:19; 8:26; 10:3) an indication that the barriers between earth and heaven are broken. Earth is about to be permeated with the radiance of celestial epiphany.

The proclamation of the Baptist's birth then is placed by Luke in the context of final preparation. The new Elias who is to herald the Messiah has reappeared. The new Samuel is here to point out the future David, and the precursor angel begins his ministry.

IV. Isaiah 49:1-6
1st reading
Feast

Exegetes discern two distinct traditions in this extract from the third Servant song. The first (vv. 1-3 and 5b-6) is the product of a universalist spirit, the second is an account of prophetic investiture. Second-Isaiah, who had seen in Cyrus the envoy of God, expresses his disillusionment. While supporting the reestablishment of Israel, the king is setting up again the temples of Mardouk and the pagan new year festivals. Accordingly, the downfall of Cyrus is proclaimed. Very soon God will send a new messenger to his people.

Having reflected on the failure of Cyrus' mission, the prophet begins to consider himself as the divine envoy that Cyrus should have been, and to eulogize his *prophetic function* in terms hitherto reserved to Cyrus. His mission will even have a universal dimension and his name will be spoken by God (v. 1; cf. Is 41:25). The sword of Cyrus which should have destroyed the king is entrusted to him (v. 2; cf. Is 41:2). He becomes the light of the nations that Cyrus would have been had he remained faithful (v. 6; cf. Is 42:16).

He sees himself called by God like Jeremiah from his conception (vv. 1 and 5; cf. Jr 1:5). His mission, like Ezechiel's, is to turn aside the sword (v. 2; cf. Ez 21:14-22). Like Jacob he must wrestle all night without failing (v. 3; cf. Gn 32:23-33). Discouraged though he is, he wants to have solidarity with his predecessors, the prophets of Israel (v. 4; cf. Jr 15:10; 20:9 and Is 49:4).

The reason for this choice of lesson for the Baptist's feast could be put as follows. Every prophet tries first of all to see God's presence and intervention in events and persons. One day, however, it becomes evident that no human situation can fully contain the divine activity. The prophet finds himself under challenge, sometimes radical challenge. It was thus with Second Isaiah, and it will be thus with the Baptist. On the eve of inauguration of the Kingdom we have an affirmation of the necessity of a radical change in attitude.

V. Acts 13:22-26
2nd reading
Feast

Here we have an extract from Saint Paul's address to the Jews in the synagogue of Antioch in Pisidia (Ac 13:16-41). It is not the most important portion (in vv. 26-29 we have the essential elements of an apostolic discourse).

The reading is chosen because of the explicit reference to the Baptist in verses 24-25.

The first part of the discourse is a resume of *salvation history* centered on the person of David and his covenant with Yahweh (vv. 17-23). The central point is found in verse 23: God has "raised up" (in the double sense of manifesting and resuscitating: cf. Ac 3:20-26; 26:6-8) for us a member of David's house as Messiah. Paul is referring to the messianic wait, and presenting the resurrection as the means chosen by God of satisfying it. In Jewish thinking faith in the resurrection was connected with messianic hope.

In this general context the Baptist is put forward by Paul as the precursor of the Messiah. His function is to prepare for the coming by proclaiming a baptism of repentance (v. 24). The reference in this instance to the Baptist indicates the anxiety of Luke to show the radical dependence of the Precursor on the Savior (v, 25; cf. Jn 1:20).

VI. Luke 1:57-66, 80
Gospel
Feast

In the account of the annunciation of the Baptist's birth (Lk 1:5-25; see the gospel of the vigil) we have all the essential traits of the Precursor. The account of the actual birth gives us nothing new. Neither birth nor circumcision (our reading, except for v. 80 which tells of the hidden life of the Baptist) are described for their own sake. The purpose is to provide a context for the imposition of the name (v. 63) which had been already proclaimed by the angel in verse 13.

The unexpected agreement between Zachary and Elizabeth is the sign that the name has been willed by heaven. The healing of Zachary's dumbness is also evidence for the bystanders that this is a *manifestation from heaven.*

The evangelist lingers to describe the joy and astonishment of the bystanders, both characteristic symptoms of the messianic times (for joy: Lk 1:14, 17, 57, 58; Ze 3:14-17; Jr 31:12-13; Is 51:3; for astonishment: Lk 1:21, 63; 2:18, 33; Ac 2:7; 3:12). The rapid spread of the news, symbolic of the rapidity of the spread of the gospel (vv. 65-66; cf. Lk 2:15, 17, 20), is likewise a sign of the presence of heaven among men.

Joy is not a necessary consequence of belief in God's presence. The God of the Jansenists, or of the pious, is not a joy-giving God. The God of joy is he whose presence is felt throughout a man's life, in secular tasks, in the most varied moods, in the most difficult encounters, in sufferings which do not lead to discouragement. Such are the joys of messianic times.

B. DOCTRINE

The Theme of Prophetism

Catholics in general have a fairly precise notion of the Church's sacramentality. This cannot be said of prophetism in the Church: for most people it is an unknown quantity. Everyone knows, it is true, that there was a series of prophets in the Old Testament, but the notion entertained of what a prophet is is singularly narrow. He is one who through divine inspiration foretells the future in veiled terms, particularly the future which concerns the Messiah. God uses such messengers to prepare his people for the salvation he is about to bestow in the sending of his own Son. With the coming of Christ however prophetism comes to an end: it is supplanted by reality.

Very few Christians seem to be aware that baptism really initiates them into a prophetic vocation, that the new covenant makes all of us prophets, enables all of us to discern God's will in the event.

It has got to be admitted that for many centuries the prophetic charism has been by no means in favor in Christian circles. There has been a long, static period where the idea of an "order" dominated everything, when it was thought to be everyone's duty to impose that order in every domain. Now we must begin to read the "signs of the times" differently. The prophetic charism must be given its opportunity, if the Church and all Christian life is not to become petrified in the structures of a dead past.

The role of prophets in Israel

The remote roots of Jewish prophetism reach into a soil that is common to neighboring peoples as well. Universally we find that certain individuals are more fitted than others to receive a message from the gods, as they discern the meaning which underlies reality. But Jewish prophetism has a further dimension that is altogether different, that depends altogether on the regime of faith. In Israel there were false prophets, no different from those to be found in other nations. Those worthy of the name were the prophets who played an active role in the establishment of the regime of faith.

Jewish prophecy is altogether concerned with the event, the point *par excellence* of encounter between God and men. Man's natural reaction to the event is to close his eyes to it, because of what it signifies in terms of the unexpected and unpredictable. He tends to search for happiness by basing himself on the solid and stable, on what is foreseeable. He wants tomorrow to be as today (Is 56:12). The prophet is one who undermines illusory securities and forces men to look on their existence with a realistic eye. He compels the chosen people to be mindful of the demands of the covenant which leads towards spiritual adventure and fidelity in the event. It is in the concrete lives of people that Yahweh intervenes to indicate his judgment and offer his salvation.

An attitude such as the prophet's makes for greater and greater interiorization. All the elements of the covenant are constantly being referred to the faith which is their basis. It is so with the Law. By recalling its precepts the prophet links it to concrete existence, and manifests the proper dynamism of this divine gift. If necessary he challenges the leaders of the people, when they corrupt the law by interpreting it in overly human terms. He contributes to a similar interiorization in matters of worship. He rejects all formalism and opens people more and more to the authentic spiritual sacrifice.

But the really great achievement of Jewish prophetism is the direction it gives to messianic hope, that backbone of the Old Testament. This comes from a keen insight into the present event, and an altogether lucid understanding of the love-relationship that God has wished to have with man from all eternity. Insofar as the "definitive today" of salvation is not realized in the present moment, the prophet summons men to turn their gaze towards the unforeseeable future. During the troubled period at the end of the monarchy particularly the prophets (see Jeremiah and Ezechiel) become the heralds of a new covenant when the Law will be graven in men's hearts. This was the moment when the mysterious figure of the suffering Servant took shape in prophetic circles. It is unquestionably the closest approximation to the Messiah who actually did come.

The fulfillment of the prophecies in Jesus Christ

It was the role of John the Baptist, the last and greatest prophet of the Old Testament, to designate the Messiah. Here we see the direct continuity between the prophetic tradition of the old covenant and the actual advent of salvation in Jesus of Nazareth. But from another angle, in the Baptist's questioning of the Messiah's attitudes, what we have emphasized is the discontinuity between the two covenants. Jesus came to fulfill the Law and the prophets, but the manner of fulfillment is unexpected. The Event *par excellence* is seen to be the salvation of man. There was one domain that the prophet's insight did not penetrate, because it could not. God's salvific initiative is expressed in the gift of his own Son: the Messiah in fact is the man-God. Reread in this light the whole prophetic quest discloses its true meaning. But that meaning lay altogether beyond the prophet's comprehension. God's plan for his creature, man, was a summons to become, in the man-God, part of his own Family. Man's yearning for the sacral was to be fulfilled beyond all dreams. The filial response to the Father's loving initiative would be expressed in terms of filial obedience to the terrestrial state after the example of Christ.

There were many things in Jesus' life that resembled the careers of Old Testament prophets. In practice however the primitive community did not use the title prophet for the Messiah. His personality completely transcended the previous prophetic tradition. Jesus in fact, because he was himself salvation, inaugurates a new prophetic tradition. He speaks not only in Yahweh's name, but in his own. "In truth, in truth I say to you": he is the salvation of which he speaks. He is the Word of God made flesh. In him are realized perfect revelation and perfect religion, prophecy and the object of prophecy. He gives the perfect answer to the Father's salvific initiative. His paschal pilgrimage is the definitive prophecy, that which leads toward the reality of salvation.

All prophets in the Church

Because she is the Body of Christ, the Church shares the prophetic charism of her Head. She is capable of reading events in the light of faith, in virtue of what has been accomplished once for all in Jesus Christ, and in view of what has still to be accomplished before the Body reaches its full stature. She too finds the event to be the place *par excellence* where the God of Jesus Christ continues to encounter man, so that the Kingdom can go on being constructed on its cornerstone.

In this prophetic charism all the members of the Church have a share, each one fulfilling his function in the body. But each one carries the responsibility of making the talent which is bestowed on him bear fruit.

From the very beginning the Church was fully conscious of this. On Pentecost day Saint Peter affirms that the Spirit, in accordance with the Scriptures, is spread throughout the community "of the final times." All are fitted to be prophets. He himself, in his first discourse, is simply putting into operation the prophetic charism. The history of the Church shows that this charism has never been absent. At every period men and women have responded in fidelity to the call of the Spirit. They have manifested to their fellow believers what the eye of faith can discern in the events of their time.

While prophetism in the Church is a universal gift, not all are prophets to the same degree. The saints have been prophetic in the highest degree, and that is why they have always seemed reformers in one or other domain. Because, if the Church is to be the light that enlightens the world, that must always be because of the authenticity of the faith to be found in her.

The exercise of the charism however ought always to be submitted to the principle of regulation. No one, however high the degree of his holiness, has within himself the guarantee of his prophetic word. Under the new Covenant there is not, and never can be, any norm of genuine prophecy other than that of Christ living in his Church. He carries out his function as Head through the ministry of the apostolic Body.

Mission the work par excellence of ecclesial prophetism

Mission becomes the work *par excellence* of ecclesial prophetism insofar as those conducting it become true witnesses of the faith. Otherwise it is liable to degenerate into mere propaganda. The object of mission is to implant the mystery of Christ in a new soil, so that before the eyes of men of every race and every social condition that light may shine, which alone is capable of fulfilling their destiny. This sort of missionary activity then is prophetic activity *par excellence*, and in every enterprise of mission something new has to be shaped, a new visage for the Church. This is the task of a faith that is ecclesial.

Missionary prophetism is concerned with reading the "signs of the times," as John XXIII has shown us so magnificently by summoning the Second Vatican Council. It is concerned with the actual world and the salvation of actual humanity. It is always the source of renewal in the Church, of "aggiornamento," and has constant actuality.

In our day the witness of faith rendered by the Church ought to be concentrated in those areas where men are becoming more and more conscious of shaping their own destiny. Christians and non-Christians work daily side by side to find answers to the great challenges of our times. There is more need than ever for the prophetic word to blossom into concrete act, if its power and transcendence is to be made manifest. Here again the example has been set for us by John XXIII. The most important documents that he has left to us cannot be separated from his prophetic acts which sometimes met with incomprehension.

Ecclesial prophetism and the eucharistic assembly

The place *par excellence* for the exercise of ecclesial prophetism is the eucharistic assembly, because there are found the conditions for full authenticity. It is, first of all, an initiation into the paschal mystery, thus fitting the participants for genuine prophetism. The single prophet of the new covenant is Jesus, and only the living link of sacramental faith in him enables believers to share his prerogative.

Secondly it makes us sharers in the Word that is proclaimed. This Word is from Jesus; it is the expression of his prophetic action. It is an essential activity of the Church, carried out through the ministry of priests. By means of it the believer comes to discern salvation in the events that touch him and his brothers. In it he finds the guarantee of his own prophetic activity.

Finally, the eucharistic celebration reminds the believer that the purpose of prophetism is always the service of the assembly, or, in broader terms still, the common good. As Saint Paul is careful to emphasize in addressing the Corinthians, authentic prophetism builds up the Church.

June 29

SAINTS PETER AND PAUL, APOSTLES

A. THE WORD

I. Acts 3:1-10
1st reading
Vigil

This passage, which recounts the cure of a paralyzed man belongs to a series of narratives (Ac 3-5) where Peter plays the principal role.

a) The account stresses above all the *thaumaturgic power* of the apostles, the sign which manifests that they are really the depositories of Jesus' messianic power. Just as the first Christians only discerned Jesus' Messiahship in the miracles he wrought for the benefit of the poorest (cf. Is 35:6), they looked for the same evidence of Messiahship in those who claimed to hold his mandate. Peter provides this evidence by his cure which is wrought not in the name of the "risen" Lord, but in that of the "Messiah," Jesus of Nazareth (v. 6: cf. Mk 9:38; 16; 17). He also, at least in the version of the miracle given by the Acts, imitates the words and gestures of Christ the healer. His command is identical with that of Jesus: "arise and walk" (v. 6: cf. Lk 5:23). His miracle takes place just where Jesus had wrought a similar cure (Mt 21:14). Finally, he takes the sick person by the hand after the manner of Jesus (v. 7; cf. Lk 8:54). However the anxiety he shows to have the gaze fixed upon him (vv. 4-5) shows how much he feels a neophyte in the exercise of his charism.

This thaumaturgic power of the apostles was thus seen by the primitive community as a sign of continuity between the time of Jesus and that of the Church. It is a guarantee that Jesus the Messiah is still present with his own on the other side of death.

b) Peter's miracle also testifies to the *reassembly* in the temple of all those hitherto excluded. He is sharing one of the preoccupations of the terrestrial ministry of his master (Mt 21:12-16). He does not yet understand that Christ's death has put a closure to the temple economy (Jr 2:13-17), and he nourishes the hope of seeing this abode of God a center of universal reassembly. The sacrificial and priestly dimensions of Jesus' death and resurrection are not yet clear to him. He is still a follower of the temple liturgy (v. 1), though he does realize that from now on the barriers excluding the unclean (Gentiles, the sick, children: cf. Lv 21:18; 2 S 5:8) from the liturgical assembly ought to be destroyed (v. 8). However unaware he be of the full implications of the death, he senses at least the universalist and missionary requirements of the new religion.

This account of Peter's miracle and the anxiety to present it as similar to those of Christ is a precious indication of the nature of primitive Christian faith. At the beginning there was little concern with a collection of sayings designed to indicate the doctrinal message of Jesus. All interest was concentrated on the person and messianic event of Jesus, something that extended beyond his death, seen in a veiled way in the action of the apostles. A belief that the thaumaturgic work of Jesus is not completed with his death presumes the belief that this death is the beginning of an unprecedented spread of his Messiahship to the multitude of those who had been excluded by the narrow boundaries of Judaism. When Peter brings the unclean man into the temple, he is proclaiming his faith in the victory over death, in a Messiahship that knows no limits.

II. Galatians 1:11-20
2nd reading Vigil

Paul is affirming that he owes his gospel to a "revelation," to a personal intervention of Christ, that is, in his life, not to the Christian community in Jerusalem (vv. 11-12). To them he is indebted for many traditions and formulas (cf. 1 Co 15:1-3); but his message belongs to the order of "apocalypse" (revelation).

a) As proof for this assertion Paul recalls the events which preceded and followed his conversion. The main fact which emerges is that Paul not only underwent a personal conversion becoming instead of an enemy a disciple. Coincident with this was a more fundamental call which made him the apostle of the Gentiles (v. 16). For him, the great results of the Damascus event were personal conversion, *apostleship* and a mission to the Gentiles.

Thus it is not because of its content that the gospel of Paul differs from that of the Twelve, but rather because of its diffusion to the Gentiles, something which, for Paul, is an integral part of his message.

b) When he makes contact with Jerusalem (v. 17: cf. Ga 2:1-2) this is not with the purpose of verifying his gospel, but in order to defend the principle of evangelizing the nations (the way to Christ was open without either law or circumcision, cf. Ga 2:6). There could be no question of disavowal by the Twelve of a gospel that came from God himself. It is to stress the *unity* of mission that Paul makes much of his association with Jerusalem. He welcomes endorsement from that quarter, not because he has the slightest hesitation about the content of his gospel, but because he fears any hindrance to unity in mission.

This reading is a particularly fortunate choice for the feast of Sts. Peter and Paul. Peter is head of the apostles, but this is not to say that the only business of the other apostles is to await directives from him. Paul here throws into relief the individual character of every apostolic charism, which is a gift of the Spirit in view of the diverse requirements of mission. Nevertheless this diversified work must be basically a single enterprise. He goes to Jerusalem not to seek absolute uniformity. He wishes to integrate into collegiality the specific course he has himself taken.

His original measures must be recognized by the other apostles as part of the one and only gospel of Christ.

III. John 21:15-19 *Gospel Virgil*

In John's gospel it is the Risen Lord who transmits his powers to the apostles (Jn 20:21-23). In particular it is in the context of apparitions of the Risen Lord that Peter receives the primacy (our reading). This is contrary to the synoptics, who place the event before Jesus' death (Mt 16:13-20, with parallel passages). The fourth gospel is concerned to show that the missionary and sacramental powers of the Church are but the radiation of the glory of the Risen Lord (cf. also Mt. 28:18-19).

The transmission of powers which takes place in this passage, consecrated to the primacy of Peter, is not without humorous aspects. As Peter had three times denied his master (Jn 18:17-27) he is now required by Jesus to make a profession of love three times. He had thought himself superior to others in his zeal for the Lord, but what Christ demands from him is superiority in love ("more than these": v. 15).

Peter does not openly affirm his attachment to the Lord: he relies humbly on the knowledge that Christ must have of this ("you know"—vv. 15-17). They are not both using love in the same sense. Twice Jesus asks if Peter loves (*agape*) him. Peter replies that he is attached (*philein*) to his master. He does not make any affirmation with regard to the religious love demanded by Jesus: he is content to indicate his attachment. Of course all the attachment and affection connoted by *philein* is to be found in *agape*, but the latter concept comprises also fidelity in the service exclusively of the Risen Lord and consecration to God (cf. Jn 14:15-24). Jesus however challenges the apostle in the domain of friendship too. In the third question he refers not to *agape*, but uses Peter's own word *philein*. "Are you really attached to me?"

The sudden change of tone and language upsets Peter. Can Christ be questioning also his attachment and affection?

In fact it will be by the exercise of his primacy, by the manner in which he loves the lambs and sheep of the Lord, that Peter will give evidence of both his affection and his *agape.*

The *agape* of Christ in his death (Jn 15:14) is henceforward an institution: the Church, led by Peter, is the visible sacrament of this *agape.* If the pastor loves his sheep as he ought, a sign of the love of Christ will be given to the world. The primacy is not a reward for the love Peter eventually showed for his master: it is an institution which manifests Christ's love for men.

IV. Acts 12:1-12
1st reading
Feast

It is probable that the account of Peter's arrest and miraculous release (Ac 12:1-19) was inserted in the Acts by a hand other than that of Luke. From the point of view of style in any case, the episode suggests Mark more than anyone.

The Jewish tradition (cf. Midrash Ex 18-81a) regarded deliverances such as that of Joseph (Gn 39:21-41:45), the three children from the furnace (Dn 3:26), or Daniel (Dn 4:24), as signs of paschal *liberation* (Ex 12:42). It is noteworthy that many features of this account suggest the Jewish pasch:

verse 3: proximity of the Pasch
verse 6: the same night (Ex 12:12 LXX)
verse 7: get up, quickly (Ex 12:11 in haste LXX)
verse 8: gird yourself and put on shoes (Ex 12:11)
verse 11: "I know . . ." (C Dn 3:95 after Theodotion)

Furthermore we have a series of items (Lk 12:35a, inspired by Ex 12:11a; 1 P 1:13; Ep 6:14, etc.) which indicate that an eschatological interpretation was given to the ritual of the paschal night. Probably it was because of this that the Christian idea developed of the coming of Christ at the dead of night (Mk 13:33; Mt 24:42; Lk 12:35; Rm 13:11; 1 Th 5:1; Rev 3:3; 16:15). Everything suggests that the Christian paschal night, like the Jewish, was regarded as the night of deliverance for the just.

Thus the significance of the account becomes clear. In order to be worthy of the plenipotentiary ministry of the Messiah, Peter must undergo the same trial and the same deliverance as his master. He becomes like Christ, for the Christian community, an example of the liberated one, a witness to the reality of paschal salvation.

V. 2 Timothy 4:6-8, 17-18
2nd reading
Feast

This passage is taken from a sort of farewell discourse by Paul to his disciple Timothy. This literary genre had a series of elements that are well exemplified in our reading: satisfaction at having accomplished properly a mission (vv. 6-7; cf. Jn 17:6, 13; Ac 20:20-21), announcement of forthcoming departure (vv. 6-7; cf. Jn 13:33; Ac 20:22-25), a fairly pessimistic view of the current situation (vv. 16-17; cf. Ac 20-22, 29-34), absolute confidence in divine aid (v. 18; cf Jn 17:13; Ac 20:24).

Paul is practically certain that this trial is going to be his last. One of the greatest troubles of his captivity is that he must undergo it in absolute isolation. In the very midst of trial he remains faithful (v. 7) to his mission. It provides him with the opportunity to converse with his pagan judges and proclaim his gospel to them. How could such a *trial* be a failure in his mission when it proves an occasion of evangelizing (v. 17)!

VI. Matthew 16:13-19
Gospel
Feast

The passage that there is general agreement in calling the "confession of Caesarea" is a fairly homogeneous one which comprises Peter's profession of messianic faith, the first announcement of the passion, a moral application (the apostles too will have to bear their cross), and finally the transfiguration. Very probably the whole piece belongs to primitive catechesis (Mt 16:13-17:9; Mk 8:27-9:10; Lk 9:18-26), though it is fairly evident that the episodes recounted took place independently of one another. Matthew's version is certainly the best; but it is very probably due to the primitive community that we have a post-paschal mission placed before the resurrection.

For a proper understanding of this text of Matthew the reading should be prolonged to verse 23. We have then the following structure:

A		B	
v. 13	address by Christ	v. 21	address by Christ
v. 16	intervention by Peter	v. 22	intervention by Peter
v. 17	thoughts of God not of men	v. 23	thoughts of men not of God
v. 18	you are the rock of the Church	v. 23	you are the rock of scandal

a) The account accordingly is centered around the double *exchange of titles* between Jesus and Peter. Peter gives Jesus the title of Messiah, and Jesus responds by giving him the name Peter together with the messianic power of the keys. Peter refuses to give Jesus the title of suffering Servant: Jesus responds by calling him the rock of scandal.

b) The title given to Jesus (v. 16) is essentially *messianic:* "you are the Christ." Matthew strengthens this by adding "the son of the living God." It does not appear that this phrase indicates Jesus' divinity strictly speaking. It is often used in the Old Testament to designate the angels (Gn 6:1-4; Jb 1:6), judged (Ps 81/82:6-7) and the king (2 S 7:14; Ps 88/89:27-28). It is then merely a doublet of the title Christ, an affirmation of the divine origin of Jesus' Messiahship. Recognition as the Messiah means recognition as the one and only person who can give meaning to life and bring it to achievement.

c) Hardly has his Messiahship been recognized when Jesus, according to Matthew at least, hastens to make Simon a sharer in it.

Immediately he gives him the messianic title *Peter* (v. 18) which will remain his personal name. He also gives him the prerogatives of invulnerability and firmness attributed to David, Sion and the Messiah (theme of the gates of hell, v. 18; cf. Is 28:16).

Then he gives him the power of the keys (v. 19). Here we have the full ambit of biblical imagery. Christ holds the keys of David's dwelling (Is 22:22). He is the major domo of the Father's house (v. 19) and entrusts Peter with this office.

Finally Peter receives the power of "binding and loosing" which he exercises in collegiality with the other apostles (Mt 18:18; cf. Jn 20:22-23). In fact the phrase, by continuing two contraries, expresses the totality of power: the apostle is a veritable plenipotentiary.

B. DOCTRINE

The Theme of Peter and Paul

The Church celebrates on the same day the feast of Saint Peter and that of Saint Paul. They are both, by different titles, members of the apostolic college. By celebrating both together, the Church reminds us that the two titles are complementary and are both necessary for the exercise of collegiality.

The Second Vatican Council has solemnly proclaimed that episcopal collegiality is something of divine right. By his consecration each bishop becomes a member of a college, which is the successor throughout history of the first apostolic college. As is usual in such circumstances the reasons swaying the council members towards collegiality were practical rather than theological. This was to be expected. Bishops are pastors and they expressed themselves in terms of the actual demands of their mission. There were two ways in which these demands suggested collegiality. On the one hand it was no longer possible for the pope to govern alone a Church that in the course of a century had become so widespread and so complex. On the other, pastoral problems confronting bishops in their territories extended further than diocesan boundaries, and demanded collective action on a regional or even continental scale. Practical though such considerations were, they were not theological reasons. If collegiality is of divine right, it has always existed in the Church, and its doctrinal basis should be understood.

This joint feast of Saints Peter and Paul provides the opportunity for reflection on the basic meaning of episcopal collegiality. We must inquire in what sense Peter and Paul form the two axes and the internal dynamism of its structure.

Episcopal collegiality and the law of Charity

We know that Jesus entrusted his Church not to one person only. At one and the same time, and in the same terms, he entrusted it at once to a college of twelve apostles, and to one among them, Peter.

This action on his part corresponded with the essential character of the salvation to be acquired in him. In founding the Church, he indicated his intention of remaining in person among his own throughout the course of history. In his resurrection he would be the one mediator of salvation, but he could only remain present with men through the ministry of special envoys consecrated for that purpose. Such a ministry of mediation could not be exercised by one only: it was impossible that a single person could appropriate to himself the ministry of the unique mediator. It was a ministry that could only be exercised by several simultaneously, once they were established in grace (this is the basic meaning of the sacrament of orders) in those bonds of charity of which Christ alone has the secret, that charity by which on the cross the salvation of the world was wrought.

Consequently the authenticity of apostolic or episcopal ministry is guaranteed by the *fraternal accord* of its members in the exercise of their charge. Because of the grace received at the imposition of hands their accord is an adequate expression of the law of charity which constitutes the Church as the Body of Christ.

The history of the Church since its origins demonstrates that this insight was never altogether lacking, but that it was not always lived with the same intensity. Saint Paul, in order that he might not run in vain, sought at all costs the support of the other apostles for his pastoral endeavors. Throughout the early centuries the successors of the apostles, who had become residential bishops, developed multiple contacts with one another in order to cement the bonds of brotherhood that would guarantee their own pastoral efforts. In the fourth century begins that series of great ecumenical councils where all the bishops were brought together to seek solutions for the major ecclesiastical problems of the time. At a very early stage the ecumenical council was seen as the institution *par excellence* of episcopal collegiality, its fullest expression. In the meantime the Church was getting established. Historical developments, which varied as between East and West, tended to make her reinforce her unity by multiplying legislation. A fraternal accord that was maintained by frequent episcopal contacts began to yield to universal observance of legislation emanating from Rome or Constantinople. Frequent episcopal contact was no longer necessary, because the bishops were constrained to follow everywhere the same procedures. Unity was indeed assured; but the image of the Church was impaired, and schism between East and West was not avoided. Furthermore, the whole missionary enterprise was hurt by the fact that it was regarded as the expansion over other areas of an "established order" characteristic of the countries of Christendom.

Subsequently a number of factors combined to create a situation where ecclesial unity could no longer be maintained by means of uniformity. We had the development in the 20th century of native bishops, the decline of Europe's primacy in the concert of nations, the challenge by atheism to ecclesial catholicity, the disestablishment of the Church in so many areas, the development, on a global scale, of contacts between nations. This was why it became essential to feature once more episcopal collegiality, the basic guarantee of catholicity and of missionary dynamism. It was the achievement of John XXIII that he understood this need, and convoked for that reason the Second Vatican Council.

Peter and the fundamental principle of episcopal collegiality

At the moment when he confided the future of his Church to the College of the Twelve, Jesus confided it to Peter as head of the college. "Thou are Peter and on this rock I will build my Church" (Mt 16:18). The basic principle of the apostolic college we have just seen to be the law of charity, which makes the Church the Body of Christ. The primacy has the very same basic principle. Seeing that the authenticity of the apostolic ministry is guaranteed by the fraternal accord between the members of the college, this accord must have some sort of visible norm of verification. This is constituted by the presence of a head in the college. His role can scarcely be better defined than in the language of Irenaeus, who sees the successor of Peter as "presiding" over charity.

Whether the pope acts alone or in company with his brothers in the episcopacy (which is the case in an ecumenical council) he always acts as head of the episcopal college, in order to cement the fraternal accord that guarantees the authenticity of the college and its members. Papal primacy is necessary for the exercise of episcopal collegiality, because it is the living touchstone of the fraternity between members of the college, which builds up the Church in the charity of Christ. The bishops realize that their communion is building up the Church when it is manifested in the successor of Peter.

It would be very wrong then to think that there are two distinct organs of supreme power in the Church, the pope and the college of bishops. The pope is himself a member of the college, and when he acts as pope he acts as head of the college. On the other hand the episcopal college does not exist without its head, and without the pope the bishops cannot constitute it.

In these years following the Second Vatican Council we shall see the establishment of various institutions designed to secure effective exercise of episcopal collegiality, particularly in the governance of the universal Church. This will be a delicate project because care will have to be taken that each has his proper place. It is nevertheless a necessary project: nothing less than ecclesial renewal is at stake.

Paul and the fundamental principle of episcopal collegiality

Fifteen years after the first Pentecost, at a time when the primitive Jerusalem community was increasing day by day, and the hellenist party had set themselves the task of evangelizing neighboring territories, the Risen Christ appeared to the Jew Saul of Tarsus, and gave him the mission of evangelizing the Gentiles. He had been a persecutor of Christians.

This calling of Saul, who took the name of Paul, was undoubtedly the most important event in the early history of the Church. His ministry was destined to establish nascent Christianity firmly in the Greek world, and to open the gates of the Church to the uncircumcised. True, the foundation of the Antioch Church by Barnabas had provided a beginning before Paul's intervention, but it was Paul's missionary journeys that laid the lines of Christian expansion throughout the Mediterranean world. His activity proved so crucial for the development of the Church in so many ways that the Christianity of subsequent centuries can well be described as a Pauline heritage.

We see him throughout long years vindicate his status as apostle on the same level as the great apostles, the members of the apostolic college. When he began to evangelize he was aware of the importance of his mission, but he was far from being a member of the apostolic college. Little by little he became more aware of the ecclesial importance of his role, and he divined that this role had to be validated at the highest ecclesiastical level. The great apostles would have to associate him with their college. Insofar as this college fails to assume responsibility for any missionary enterprise, it is proving false to its fundamental principle.

Such is the lesson we learn from the Pauline experience. In this first apostolic college, it was not one of the Twelve, but an unexpected member of the Diaspora, called in unprecedented fashion by the Risen Lord himself, who most vigorously fostered missionary zeal. It is to the credit of the Twelve that they associated themselves with a person of such quality.

The primitive experience of the Church was to be verified throughout its long history. The Risen Lord calls whom he pleases when he wants to restore missionary vigor in his Church according to the needs of the time. Every member of his Body, even a non-Christian, may be the subject of this call. It is the business of the episcopal college to associate themselves always with such people, for whom missionary responsibility is everything. We have had priests and laity whose whole lives have been dominated by the needs of mission.

Whenever the episcopal college has failed in this task, missionary enterprises that were at once daring and necessary ended in collapse. The most notable instance was the Jesuit enterprise in China at the end of the 16th century. The evangelization of this country required new methods: the mission had to meet the challenge of a great, profoundly humanized, nation to whom the faith had nothing to contribute on the purely cultural plane. There could be no question of transporting there the Christian "order" of the Western world. All that was needed was the proclamation of the Good News, and the Jesuits gave themselves resolutely to this task. Many popes recognized them as excellent laborers in the field of the Lord. Yet their enterprise finally issued in failure. We believe the basic reason for this lies in the fact that the enterprise was never fully integrated into the episcopal college itself, and hence into the whole ecclesial body. In the essential sense, Western Christianity, pope, bishops and faithful, remained untouched by this new Pauline manifestation.

The missionary situation of the Church today resembles in more than one respect that of Saint Paul's time. Certainly the challenges to catholicity are of the same magnitude. To meet them it will not be sufficient for the episcopal college to follow ordinary means of action, and for Peter's successor merely to fulfill his normal structural role. We shall have to have in the episcopal college men of Pauline stature, whose task it will be to have the college as a whole stand behind the sort of daring missionary initiatives that are imperative at this time.

August 6

TRANSFIGURATION OF THE LORD

A. THE WORD

I. Daniel 7:9-10, 13-14 *1st reading*

Chapter 7 of Daniel is one of the most important apocalyptic texts in the whole Bible. The golden age of apocalyptic literature began in the second century B.C., at a period, that is, when the faith was under serious challenge. There would have to be a final confrontation between God and the pagan world, since God himself had been challenged by Antiochus Epiphanes (175-163). The prophet Daniel in a dream sees four symbolic beasts emerging from the sea and mounting the earth. They represent the kingdoms which successively threatened Israel: the Babylonian empire, the kingdom of the Medes, the Persian kingdom, and finally that of Alexander and his successors, one of whom was Antiochus Epiphanes. At this point there intervenes a mysterious figure, juxtaposed with God in a scene that is preliminary to the definitive judgment (our reading today).

The thrones of the judges (v. 9) are placed around the throne of Yahweh and the books in which all human acts are written (v. 10) are open. A mysterious personage for whom the clouds provide a heavenly chariot (v. 13) approaches God. He is depicted as a "Son of Man," a sort of celestial double for the ideal Israel, which is itself described further on as "the people of saints of the Most-High" (Dn 7:18, 22, 25, 27). What the prophet wants to emphasize touches on the essential core of Jewish hope. A day will come when the true people of God will be established. In this context however the establishment is made from on high, and is therefore unprecedented.

The Son of man then in Daniel 7 has primarily a collective and transcendent meaning. We can however ask ourselves whether the notion of the *Messiah* is not included in the author's vision, or at least something very closely approaching that. Just as the four pagan kingdoms are concentrated in their beings (Dn 7:17), so are the people of saints in their head, the Messiah. It was thus in any event that the text was understood in subsequent tradition (cf. Enoch 37-41; 2 Esdras 13 and the most constant rabbinic tradition). In the time of Jesus Daniel's prophecy was thought to apply to a person who mysteriously transcended the ordinary human state.

Jesus put himself forward as the Son of man foretold by the prophet Daniel. By contrast however with the presentiment of Daniel, he shared completely the ordinary human condition. The glory that was manifested at his transfiguration is not that of some transcendent extraordinary creature. It was that of a man, destined like all men for death, whom men had failed to recognize with the eyes of faith as the very Son of God. Because of that it was a divine glory.

II. 2 Peter 1:16-19 *2nd reading* The primary object of this letter is to remind readers of the true doctrine concerning the Parousia. At the time of writing there were numerous gnostic objections concerning delays in the Lord's return. To these the author opposes true knowledge of Christ (2 P 1:2, 3, 8; 2:20; 3:18), that which rests on apostolic witness and the word of prophecy (today's reading).

From apostolic witness the author cites a single event, the Transfiguration (vv. 16-18). The details given are taken from evangelic tradition; but for the author its main importance is that it is a prelude to the glorious manifestation of Christ at the end of time, of which it is the first indication.

He regards the word of prophecy (v. 19) as the most solid argument for the *Parousia.* Apostolic witness is a confirmation only. He does not nevertheless refer to a specific text for this. All of Scripture, with the authority conferred on it by the inspiration of the Holy Spirit (2 P 1:20-21) speaks in favor of the *Parousia.*

The choice of this reading for the Transfiguration feast is not purely arbitrary, though it does not have an immediately obvious apologetic dimension. It reminds us of the basic truth of faith that all human history, but especially that of Jewish hope, leads to the fuller manifestation of the mystery of Christ. It is thus that we begin to see its genuine meaning.

III. Luke 9:28b-36 *Gospel*

Luke's account of the Transfiguration does not concentrate so much on the phenomenon itself. Doubtless he feared that readers of pagan background would confuse it with the "metamorphoses" of mythology. Thus he merely says that the aspect of Jesus' countenance changed, and makes this the result of his prayer (vv. 28b-29). Furthermore with the glory of Jesus (v. 31) he associates first of all Moses and Elias, then the apostles themselves (v. 34), thus modifying to some extent the originality of the episode.

He lays more emphasis than the other evangelists on the presence of Moses and Elias. He is the only one to mention their particular glory and to give particulars of the exchange between Jesus and Moses and Elias, the "exodus" of the Lord, that is (v. 31, badly rendered generally as "departure").

a) The determining element in Luke's account seems to be Jesus' prayer to his Father (vv. 28b-29). Luke likes to place such a prayer at the most decisive moments of Jesus' life, the Transfiguration being one. Jesus has just become aware of the failure of his mission, and his presentiment of an imminent death resembles that of the leader of a revolutionary band (Lk 9:22). He also has the presentiment that those of his disciples who want to follow him to the end will likewise pay with their lives for their messianic enthusiasm (Lk 9:23-26). Is not this the real moment of union with God? Even before he mounts the cross, Jesus is already dead, dead to the mission he thought he would accomplish, dead to ambitions for influence and success, dead maybe to the concept of a God who arranges everything and accomplishes miracles in his favor. His prayer then was an offering of himself just as he was to God, the discovery of a new visage of God, one that is seen only after death when all securities have been undermined. The exterior transfiguration of Jesus could only be the reflection of a deep interior certitude, the conviction that God is always there, beyond the hazards of death and total failure. He is all the more ready to glorify Jesus and his disciples, to the extent that they have totally relinquished all pursuit of human glory.

b) It is certain that Luke saw in Jesus the fulfillment of the prophecy of Deuteronomy 18:15 where a successor of his own ilk is promised to Moses. The prophecy frequently recurs in his writing (v. 35b; cf. Ac 3:22; 7:37). Jesus is for him, as he is for Matthew, a second Moses (cf. Lk 14:27). He goes further than Matthew however in showing that Jesus is inaugurating the *new "Exodus"* (v. 31). The Exodus from Egypt had been in the Old Testament, the model of God's intervention in salvation history. If he were to intervene again, that could only be in the way of a new Exodus (Mi 7:15; Is 11:11). For Luke this new Exodus begins from the terrestrial Jerusalem, which is like ancient Egypt unbelieving (Mk 19:41-44; 13:33-34; 21:37) and wends towards the new Jerusalem (cf. Ga 4:25-26; He 12:22), the dwelling of the Father, passing through a "submersion" in the sea (Lk 12:50). Jesus is in fact from the transfiguration onwards *en route* towards "Jerusalem," a stage that he will only complete by quitting the ancient capital for the mount of olives and the ascension (Ac 1:6-11). Curiously enough, the principal stages of this Exodus, the transfiguration (v. 30), the resurrection (Lk 24:4, though here the other evangelists speak of one person only) and the ascension (Ac 1:10) are marked by the presence of "two witnesses." Are not these, in each case, Moses and Elias?

Thus Luke takes a middle way between Matthew and Mark. Where Matthew sees in the episode above all the revelation of the new Moses as legislator of the new covenant, and Mark is chiefly sensitive to the events of the Lord's Pasch, he keeps both perspectives. He makes Jesus the new Moses indeed, but also a legislator who seals a new covenant in the accomplishment of his personal Exodus.

The presence of Moses and Elias by the side of Jesus can have a more important meaning still for modern man. In ancient Israel these two patriarchs had vainly tried to pierce the mystery of God without reaching it (Ex 3; 1 K 19). But now in Jesus their quest is ended. The mystery of God is perceived insofar as God reveals himself in his humanity, for the service of men. The quest of the patriarchs is constantly being guided towards the reality of God in history, something that was to culminate in Jesus. There could be no return to Sinai or Horeb. The only possible journey's end was Jesus, perfect God and perfect man, totally at the service of men. Perhaps the transfiguration is less the mystery of Jesus' individual divinization than the discovery by men of the God who serves them, a God unknown to the philosophers.

B. DOCTRINE

A doctrinal meditation on the transfiguration will be found on the second Sunday of Lent under the title "The Law and Moral Life" (Vol. III, pp. 80-84).

August 15

ASSUMPTION OF THE VIRGIN MARY

A. THE WORD

I. 1 Ch 15:3-4, 15-16; 16:1-2
1st reading
Vigil

The story of the transference to Jerusalem of the ark of the covenant (1 Ch. 15:1-16:3) had been already told in 2 Samuel 6:12-19. Its rereading in the third century B.C. by the author of Chronicles stresses the liturgical dimension. At the time of writing the Jerusalem temple had become the center of Israel's life, having lost as she had, after the exile, her political structures. The leaders were the priests and Levites, assisted by a whole series of subordinates. For the author, David was the king *par excellence:* the community should live according to his spirit.

Ever since Sinai, until the construction of the temple where it would be definitively installed, the *ark of the covenant* constituted in Israel's eyes the sign *par excellence* of God's presence among his people. It contained the ten commandments written on stone by God himself (Dt 10:1-5), and was thus a sanctuary where Yahweh himself could reside.

Because she was a nation of faith, it was altogether natural for Israel to see in the ark of the covenant the place where Yahweh manifested his active presence. He had led his people through the desert to the conquest of the Promised Land (cf. Nb 10:33; Ex 15:3; 1 S 4:22); but, as the history of the ark itself shows, he had never allowed himself to be altogether annexed by his people (1 S 4-6). His active presence in the ark is connected with the fact that it is the place *par excellence* of his word. The Word is engraved on the tables of the Law where Yahweh has revealed his will (Ex 31:18), and continues to reveal himself (Ex 25:22). The ark is also the symbol of Israel's response to that word (Dt 31:26-27): around about it Israel continues to pray to her God (1 S 1:9; 2 S 7:18).

The particular arrangement in our reading simplifies as much as possible the ceremonial of transfer of the ark to Jerusalem. The purpose is to indicate that Mary can be considered the ark of the new alliance, because she has received into her body the One who founded it, in whose person it is concentrated. Furthermore the transfer to Jerusalem suggests the assumption of the Virgin to the veritable city of God, the definitive Jerusalem.

II. 1 Corinthians 15:54-57
2nd reading
Vigil

This is the doxology which concludes Paul's long dissertation on the resurrection of the body (1 Co 15:1-57).

Paul has set forth a specifically Christian doctrine in a Jewish context. The *resurrection* expected by the Jews was basically no more than a recovery of the physical body, in order to participate in the kingdom which would itself be material (1 K 17:17-24). The Lord's Pasch however had enabled Paul to transcend this view. The resurrection would not be a simple recovery of the body, but the body's transformation and conformation to the glorified body of Christ. The Christian view of the resurrection then differs from the rabbinic, and Paul is led to this view by his doctrine of "being with Christ." Since it means more than just the recovery of a dead body, and entails access to a new, spiritual corporeity, it is as important for the living as the dead. In order to be "with Christ," both the living and the dead will undergo a transformation, according to the state in which the Parousia will find them.

The doxology itself might well serve as a hymn on the lips of those arisen in victory over death and sin, a hymn of all humanity which has at last attained the state promised for it.

III. Luke 11:27-28
Gospel
Vigil

This short passage comes from an ensemble (Lk 11:14-32) which is lacking indeed in unity, but where the parallelism is evident. To the cure of the deaf-mute (v. 14) corresponds the beatitude for those who hear the Word (our passage, vv. 27-28). To the demand for an extraordinary sign (v. 16) corresponds the proclamation of the sign of Jonas (vv. 29-32). To the discussion about the relationship between Christ and Satan (vv. 17-20), and the parable of the strong man (vv. 21-22), corresponds the return in force of the unclean spirit (vv. 24-26). Central in the whole ensemble is the saying of Jesus "he that is not with me is against me" (v. 23).

Behind this whole ensemble lies the Jewish concept of the two spirits. The world is at the mercy of the spirit of evil and men follow the path indicated by this, but the final times will see the appearance of a new spirit, that of good, which will turn men again towards good. By expelling the demons Jesus is showing that the spirit of good has appeared in the world. The two forces are locked in merciless combat. It is the business of a man to choose one or other force.

The cure of the deaf-mute, and the beatitude on those who hear the Word, stem apparently from some source which is influenced by a catechumenal rite (cf. the "finger of God" in v. 20). The Christian, or the Christian to be, is summoned to reject the spirit of evil and choose that spirit which, by means of *obedience to the Word,* leads to new life.

Taken from their context and incorporated in the liturgical formulary of the Assumption, our two verses emphasize the fact that the Virgin Mary is blessed, not because she was the mother of

Jesus according to the flesh, but because she was the one who was the perfect listener to the Word of God. The true relationship between Jesus and his mother is that which is forged by a common obedience to the Word.

IV. Revelation 11:19a; 12:1-6a; 10ab
1st reading
Feast

This reading juxtaposes elements which do not belong to the same context. Verse 19 of chapter 11 goes with verses 1-13 of that chapter. The temple of God is the Church (as distinct from the temple of Jerusalem) and, according to Jewish tradition (2 M 2:5-8), the ark of the covenant is to reappear when the kingdom of God is established. The verses from chapter 12 belong to a group of prophecies which we find throughout chapters 12-16. They foretell the preliminaries to the Great Day of Anger. Our verses are concerned with the vision of the Woman and the conflict of the Dragon with her and her descendants (Rev 12:1-6).

The Woman in splendor—sun, moon and twelve stars are traditional images—symbolizes the *people of God*, originally Israel from which Jesus according to the flesh was born, and now the new Israel, the Church, the body of Christ. Both are beset by the persecutions of the Dragon, Satan that is, here described with the attributes of his domination. The male child to whom the Woman gives birth is manifestly the Messiah, envisioned at once historically, and also mystically in Christians themselves. Reference is made to the Ascension and to Christ sitting at the right hand of the Father (v. 6), signs of the definitive fall of Satan. The Woman flees to the desert where God has prepared a refuge for her, and the Church flees far from the world to preserve herself from the onset of the Demon. Since Old Testament times, the desert had been considered the traditional refuge of the persecuted (cf. 1 K 17:3-6; 1 M 2:29).

Verse 10, which is added to our reading, describes the victory of God and domination by his Messiah, once archangel Michael and the angels have conquered the Dragon (vv. 7-9).

The association of this text with the Virgin Mary is traditional. Both Saint Augustine and Saint Bernard saw the Woman of Revelation as a symbol for Mary, though this was foreign to the purpose of the author. All scriptural texts indeed referring to the mystery of the Church can be applied to the Virgin Mary, in that she is intimately associated with, and clarifies, the mystery of the Church, as the Second Vatican Council reminds us.

The association with her of the ark of the covenant (Rev 11:19) is a theme that we have seen in the first reading for the vigil.

V. 1 Corinthians 15:20-26
2nd reading
Feast

This is one of the most complex passages in chapter 15 of the first letter to the Corinthians. Paul is elaborating his doctrine concerning the resurrection of the dead. He is addressing an audience who believe in the immortality of the soul and regard death as a liberation of the soul from the material and corruptible body. He defends the Jewish concept of a unified person. Man is not composed of a soul and body: he is a unity, a person who realizes that since Christ's resurrection God will bestow eternal life upon him.

Verses 22:23 give us the conclusion of this argument. Verses 24-28 are a digression which describe the relation between the reign of Christ and that of the Father. Paul was doubtless anxious to show the total submission of Christ to his Father. He did not want the Corinthians to see this relationship in terms of pagan myths, where a plurality of gods, or opposed gods, were worshiped together.

a) For a proper understanding of this text we must remember the main lines in the structure of Jewish apocalypse, where the *messianic kingdom* is seen as a transition towards the reign of God. It was thus that Jewish theology was able to resolve the apparent contradiction between oracles foretelling the reign of a Messiah and those which spoke rather of a theocracy.

Paul supposes a succession between the two kingdoms, the messianic and the theocratic, but he stresses the fact that the messianic kingdom will have its special function and be of fairly long duration, sufficiently long for the Messiah to conquer all his enemies (Ps 109/110:1), including death (v. 25). In fact death, and the forces controlling the world (the celestial "powers," v. 24), would have to be submitted to the lordship of Christ (cf. Rev 20:14; 1 Co 15:54). Consequently the "end" would not be yet: a good deal of time must elapse before it could be enjoyed.

b) The New Testament does not decide concerning the issue of the combat between Christ and the *powers of the world* (v. 24), among them death. Some authors regard the combat as terminated by the resurrection of Christ (Ep 1:22; 1 P 3:22): others consider it to be consistently in progress (Ac 2:35; He 1:13; 2:8; 10:13). In the first hypothesis believers could take the view that everything had been achieved at the moment of baptism, which made them sharers in the victory of Christ. The second hypothesis, which is that of Saint Paul in this instance, would make all human life a ceaseless struggle against the forces of evil and alienating powers. It behoved the Corinthians accordingly to be careful with regard to spiritual charisms (1 Co 12-14) and their sexual lives (1 Co 7). Charisms were indeed fruits of the Kingdom, but they were no indication that perfection had been attained or the victory won.

VI. Luke 1:39-56
Gospel
Feast

The account of the visitation (vv. 39-45) and the Magnificat which is associated with it (vv. 46-55) is perfectly suited to the feast of the Assumption, the themes evoked being above all themes of victory.

a) The visitation narrative suggests the *transfer of the ark of the covenant* to Jerusalem (2 S 6:2-11). Mary, like the ark, goes to the country of Judah, towards Jerusalem (v. 39; cf. 2 S 6:2). Her journey produces the same manifestations of joy (vv. 42 and 44; cf. 2 S 6:2), even sacred "dances" (v. 44 where the infant "leaps" in his mother's womb; cf. 2 S 6:12). She stays in the house of Zachary, as the ark did in that of Obed-Edom (2 S 6:10), and is like the ark a source of blessings (v. 41; cf. 2 S 6:11-12). Elizabeth's "cry" of welcome reproduces almost literally David's words before the ark (2 S 6:9). Finally, like the ark, Mary remains three months in the house of her hosts (v. 56; cf. 2 S 6:11).

All this somewhat *recherché* symbolism conforms to the central idea of Luke. For him the circumstances surrounding the birth of Jesus are a fulfillment of both the prophecy of Malachi 3 (the coming of Yahweh to his temple) and that of Daniel 9 (the seventy weeks before the apparition of God). Already in the person of Gabriel (M1 3:1 and Lk 1:5-25) God had sent his angel into the temple: he had now to manifest his own presence there (Ml 3:2). Mary's journey to the house of Elizabeth is the first stage in fulfillment of the prophecies. The second, the ascent to Jerusalem strictly speaking (Lk 2:22-38), will be accomplished by the official presentation of the child in the temple.

b) The ark of the covenant symbolizes above all God's presence among his people, but it also led the people into battle. Thought of it suggests a warlike atmosphere, and Mary becomes the *victorious woman*. Verse 42, where Elizabeth blesses her cousin and the child she bears, recalls the acclamations addressed to Jael (Jg 5:2-31) and Judith (Jdt 13:17-18; 15:9-10) after victories over the enemy. Thus Mary is put forward here as the woman who assures her people definitive victory over evil. She inaugurates the messianic era where sin and misfortune will be abolished.

c) The *Magnificat* (see the literary analysis in Vol. I, p. 168) makes Mary the personification of the *eschatological Israel* of the poor, the veritable seed of Abraham who gain the promises. Such a function makes her the image and spokeswoman of the

Church itself. Much of the phraseology of the *Magnificat* is to be found indeed in the vocabulary of the primitive community as it celebrates its own mystery (cf. the word "exalt" in Lk 1:46, 48 and Ac 5:13; the word "savior" in Lk 1:47, 69, 71, 77 and Ac 4:12; 5:31; 13:47; Psalm 88/89:11 in Lk 1:51 and Ac 2:30; Lk 1:52 and Ac 2:22-38; 3:13). The eucharistic assembly, the concentration of eschatological Israel and the object of the promises made to Abraham, has every right then to appropriate the *Magnificat* to itself.

B. DOCTRINE

The Theme of the Assumption

For many Catholics, the proclamation in 1950 of the dogma of the Assumption seems to be something exclusively concerned with Marian piety, so characteristic of the Catholic Church. Some indeed regretted the definition, finding it inopportune in the actual context of ecumenism. Protestants of course in particular are always ill at ease when confronted by what they consider exaggerations of Marian cult.

The truth is that the ordinary brand of Catholic Mariology is too liable to regard the assumption as another glorious title to be added to the accepted privileges of the Virgin Mary. This is not the fundamental consideration: it is secondary to salvation history. The matter of basic importance in Marian dogma is Mary's role in the accomplishment of the Father's salvific plan. This is not an isolated or extraordinary role: it throws a clear light on the general conditions for the response of faith. Marian dogma is closely linked to the mystery of the Church: both mutually clarify each other.

The Assumption of Mary is a dogma particularly suited to the apostolic needs of our time, though its opportuneness in this particular way has been little emphasized. That the first of believers should be enjoying here and now the definitive victory over death, which affects the body as well as the soul, is a matter of direct interest in the evangelization of the world. Nothing so much concerns the world nowadays as the destiny of the body and the cosmos. If we have a clearer understanding of the dogma of the Assumption, our understanding of Christianity itself will be considerably deepened.

Yahweh's victory in Mary's poverty

The covenant between Yahweh and his people shows that his victory in the accomplishment of his plan for men is linked to the people's response.

Throughout the whole history of the chosen people, the Bible informs us that several women had a privileged role in the fulfillment of divine intentions. We have the case of Judith for example (Jdt 13). She contributed to Israel's victory over her enemies, and her intervention was a signal manifestation to everyone that this victory was a victory of Yahweh himself. Her resources were feeble compared to those of Holophernes, but the essential thing is that Yahweh is on her side. His power is manifested in her weakness. True, she is a courageous woman, not as other women. She has the characteristics of a national heroine. The idea of divine salvation that was then entertained was still too closely linked with the political prestige of Israel.

Mary on the other hand is no national heroine. She is a woman of common origin. Nothing distinguishes her from her fellow women except the quality of her hope. She sees the accomplishment of God's plan not in a victory of arms, but in a radical conversion of hearts. The Covenant is not something which gives Israel a special privilege, but something which imposes a special responsibility. Everything is turned towards the future: God will cause to issue from the human heart the act which saves Israel, and consequently all humanity.

Mary's hope is linked to her poverty. She could say with absolute truth "I am the handmaid of the Lord." So stripped of self is her faith that she is ready for the unpredictable, the impossible in terms of human wisdom. Poor as she is, she anticipates nothing from herself. She realizes that salvation does not depend on the quality of her faith or her virtue: on the contrary it depends altogether on divine benevolence and God's liberating intervention. Her faith is open to all the universalist dimensions.

In this poverty of the young girl from Nazareth is about to be wrought the great victorious exploit of Yahweh. On the day of the Annunciation she becomes the mother of the Savior, God's own son. Thanks to her whose faith can be expressed in a never-ending *Magnificat* (see today's gospel) the history of salvation strictly speaking is inaugurated.

Jesus' victory over death and Mary's Assumption

The son of Mary is the real partner in the Covenant: in his hands God's salvific plan is brought to accomplishment. From one angle everything is completed on the day of the Incarnation, but the accomplishment will require a long pilgrimage of obedience unto the death of the cross. Death is conquered on his own territory: Jesus' victory is one of love over hate.

Sealed by her divine maternity, Mary's faith led her ceaselessly along the path traced by her son. From the Annunciation until Golgatha she accompanied him. At the foot of the cross she fully shared the apparent failure of the Messiah. She did not always understand what she witnessed, but she never protested. Constantly her faith adjusted itself to the Father's will. The events he had to encounter were sadly mysterious; their meaning was hidden in God's love. By the insight of her faith Mary was already contributing to human salvation. Behind the whole sorrowful pilgrimage to the cross the outline of the resurrection could be discerned. Saint John who recounts the passion of Jesus under the sign of the resurrection is careful to give us that small episode where Christ on the cross confides to his mother the disciple whom he loved. At that very moment of the act which redeemed all humanity, Mary's maternity too takes on a universal dimension.

We have no mention in the gospels of an apparition by the Risen Lord to his mother. Is there not some deep meaning in this? There was no need, as there was in the case of the apostles, for a deepening and purifying of Mary's faith during the fifty days preceding Pentecost. From Easter morning onwards she understood the lesson of the Scriptures. Of course the Messiah she had in her heart awaited, that heart which was consecrated to God, had to pass by the way of death in order to triumph definitively over hate and accomplish human salvation. From the resurrection onwards she was ready for Pentecost. The Spirit had descended on her in the "yes" of the Annunciation.

On the day when she too confronted death, Jesus' victory became hers too. In his case the victory was total: the conqueror of death arose in the body. So pure was Mary's faith that she was able to experience this totality too. Her glorification extended to her body as well. The dogma of the Assumption proclaims precisely this, and adds nothing to divine maternity.

The Church's victory in Mary's Assumption

When, following Saint Paul, we describe the Church as the "Body of Christ," we are stating a fundamental truth: that the Church is radically dependent on the mystery of Christ. So close is the link that, were it to be broken, the Church would collapse into nothingness. Other New Testament expressions, however—the Church the spouse of Christ for instance—stress the fact that in this bond of unity the Church preserves a certain otherness. She is not just purely and simply Christ, but distinct from him. This illustrates the truth that all members of the Church are summoned to play a unique and irreplaceable role in the construction of the Kingdom. They bring to the passion of Christ a necessary contribution for the completion of the structure.

In concluding his reflection about the Church, Saint Paul shows perfect awareness of this otherness. With him indeed the theme of the Body is one that evolves, Christ being presented as henceforward the Head (Ep 1:22; Col 1:18). In the letters of the captivity he uses the term "plenitude" to describe the Church (Ep 1:23). The triumph of Christ, who sits at the right hand of the Father, becomes that of the Church. Such is Christ's love for the Church: "He sacrificed himself for her, to make her holy. He made her clean by washing her in water with a form of words, so that when he took her to myself she would be glorious, with no speck or wrinkle or anything like that but holy and faultless" (Ep 5:25-27).

This is the ecclesial context against which we must contemplate the assumption of Mary. Once we realize that a member of the Body of Christ shares his victory to the extent of being glorified in her own body, the Pauline image becomes strikingly vivid. The Church all resplendent, holy and immaculate is an actual fact; it is not reserved until the end of time. In one of her members accomplishment is present. This is more than just the reflection of Christ's resurrection: the glorified body of the Virgin is an independent reality.

So we see the sense in which Mary is the living image of the Church: her mystery can be described as equivalent to that of the Church. They shed light one upon the other. Everything said concerning the Church in Scripture can be applied to Mary, and *vice versa* (this, with other considerations, is the reason for liturgical application of texts). Mary's powerful intercession has this as basis: her body enjoys the glorification of the kingdom. Her intercession "for us poor sinners" has the amplitude of that of the Church itself. When we turn to Mary, we turn to the Church.

The Assumption and the missionary task of our time

One of the major concerns of mission, in our day, is the inclusion in its purview of the redemption of the whole cosmos. Our contemporaries are very sensitive to those verses in chapter 8 of Saint Paul's letter to the Romans: "creation looks forward in hope to the revelation of the sons of God"; she hopes "to be herself delivered from the servitude of corruption and enter the liberty of the glory of the sons of God" . . . "all creation until now groans in travail" (Rm 8:19, 21, 22).

The prodigious increase in man's power over nature makes the Christian aware of his responsibility in building the Kingdom here below. If he follows Christ in fidelity to the creatural state, if he obeys the Father's will unto death, the death of the cross if need be, if he practices the law of universal charity in a love that goes to the very limits, this can never be something altogether of himself. It finds its ultimate source in the Spirit and conversion of heart, and it makes for the transformation and humanization of the cosmos. The destiny of the cosmos is interwoven with human destiny: for both the future that is coming to birth entails a passage from death to life, and this is the responsibility in Jesus Christ of all humanity. The cosmos is more than the material scene where man must work out his eternal destiny. It awaits a "liberation" which will enable it to share in "the liberty of the glory of the sons of God."

This is another way of saying that the resurrection of the body is involved with a redemption of the whole cosmos. The fact that the Virgin Mary has been bodily assumed into heaven indicates that around the Risen Christ, who is the pivot of emancipated creation, the great work has already at one point reached completion. The Assumption of Mary proves to us that the resurrection of Christ is not just a consequence of his divinity. It is the central goal towards which all creation is ultimately moving.

The Eucharist as a communion with the glorified Mary

In the person of Christ and in the name of the assembled faithful, the priest proclaims the great eucharistic prayer in communion with Mary and all the saints of heaven. What relevance to this does the Assumption of Mary have?

When we share in the great thanksgiving of Christ who died for us and rose again, with certainty in our belief that the first of Church believers is already glorified in body, we begin to understand how profound our roles are as collaborators in the construction here below of the Kingdom. The Spirit is at work in the eucharistic celebration, not only for the transformation of the interior man, but for the transformation of the body too. Such will be the result of our sharing Christ's body.

That which we receive in the Eucharist will enable us in our daily lives to become agents of liberation and renewal for all creation. In this celebration the ultimate destiny of the cosmos is involved. Those with eyes to see, who participate in a genuine fashion, will find the Mass a major event in salvation history, leading towards the redemption of the world.

September 14

EXALTATION OF THE HOLY CROSS

A. THE WORD

I. Numbers 21:4b-9 *1st reading*

The brazen serpent, more exactly the "burning serpent" (*saraph*, which was to give us the word seraphim) was probably a relic of an idolatrous fertility cult preserved in the temple up to the reform of Ezechias (2 K 18:4). It must have been very popular, in that prophets and legislators made no attempt to remove it earlier from Yahweh's sanctuary.

Failing the suppression of the *brazen serpent* in the temple, it remained only that it be exorcised and integrated into the national history of Exodus. That doubtless is the purpose of the passage in today's liturgy. The author recalls one of the numerous crises of faith undergone in the desert and notes its coincidence with a ravaging malady, doubtless caused by the inroads of venomous serpents (vv. 5-7). He then describes the intercession of Moses which put an end to the trial, not so much by means of the brazen serpent as by an appeal to the faith of the people (v. 9).

Later, when the author of the book of Wisdom alludes to the brazen serpent (Wi 16:6), all trace of magic will have disappeared. In his account, our author contrasts the very different reaction of the Jews to the Egyptians when confronted with an identical plague. The latter succumbed to the fatal beasts because they did not have faith, or a mediator to deal with the malady. The Jews on the other hand finally found enough faith to be converted, and above all they could count on a mediator.

Spiritualized in this fashion, the symbol of the brazen serpent could survive among the primitive Christian communities. For them henceforward Moses and the brazen serpent became fused in the figure of Jesus raised on the cross (Jn 3:13-16; 12:32). But now more than ever faith is required from those who wish to benefit from the salvation of Christ (1 Co 10:9-10).

The choice of this particular reading for the feast of the Exaltation of the Cross will only be justified if those responsible for the liturgy consciously try to place it in salvation history. It is evident that the symbol of itself can no longer have much meaning for the modern Christian.

II. Philippians 2:6-11
2nd reading

This is a hymn to the kenosis and glorification of the Lord. It is probably of pre-Pauline origin. One can discern three strophes:

Verses 6-7a: two mentions of God; contrast between the state of godhead and that of a slave: theme "he emptied himself."

Verses 7bc-8: two mentions of man: theme "he lowered himself."

Verses 9-11: contrast between slave and Lord, between the state of obedience and of exaltation. The exaltation and the gift of the Name correspond to verse 9, as the genuflection and confession do to verses 10-11.

The contrast between the godhead and *servile condition* of Jesus does not, in Paul's mind, affirm that Jesus abandoned divinity, or that his manhood was merely appearance. The problem of the two natures is not raised in the passage. Thus in the first strophe it is not said that Jesus was God, but simply that he was equal to God. In the second Jesus' humanity is not denied: the affirmation is rather that the Lord allowed himself to be identified with men (v. 7; cf. Rm 8:3). He could have appeared on earth as Lord, claiming divine honors, but he did not do so. A theme dear to Saint Paul is that our charity ought to be impregnated with this self-renunciation of which Jesus has given us a living example (2 Co 8:9; Ga 4:1-5; He 11:24-26).

The hymn sometimes alludes to the suffering servant (compare v. 8 with Is 53:7, 10, 12). It adds to the image however the contrast "Lord-slave" and the typically biblical "lower-elevate" (Mt 23:12; Lk 1:52; 18:14; 2 Co 11:7).

The gradual descent into humiliation is paralleled by a *triumphal ascension* into glory. This image too goes beyond that of the servant who was "elevated" only (Is 52:13). Christ will transcend this. He will receive the title of Lord (Ps 109/110), one which merits the honor of "genuflection" and "proclamation," procedures reserved to God alone. Kings would indeed prostrate themselves before the suffering servant, but "because of Yahweh" (Is 49:7). When men prostrate themselves before Christ, it will be as before God, but not without simultaneous honor to the Father.

This christological hymn in Philippians may possibly be presenting Christ as a replica of Adam. In fact the word generally translated by "condition" (*morphe*) could well be the Greek version of the Hebrew word for image (cf. Gn 1:26). Christ would be the image of God as Adam was, but would not have availed himself of this title, as Adam did, to make himself the equal of God (v. 6; cf. Gn 3:5). This would support that exegesis which fails to find in the hymn a definition of Christ's divine nature. We should be dealing simply with a parallel between *Adam and Christ,* the pride and disobedience of the former contrasted with the humanity and willingness to serve of the latter. The hymn would be praising Jesus for having been faithful to the end of his human condition, death included, whereas Adam wanted to be unfaithful and thus escape death. The one destined to be affirmed the equal of God is precisely he who shows himself faithful to his human state.

Our liturgy today invites us to regard the cross as the place *par excellence* where the Lord's glory is manifested. It was this decisive moment in Jesus' life which led his disciples to confess his divinity. God's only way of revealing himself to man and giving him salvation, is the way of universal love, in full obedience to the human state.

III. John 3:13-17 *Gospel*

These verses are taken from the conclusion provided by the evangelist to the discourse of Jesus with Nicodemus (Jn 3:1-12). This is John's usual style. After one or other episode, he will give some mysterious sayings of Jesus, which he rounds off and retouches so that his readers can discern there the principal themes of his gospel.

The discourse was concerned with faith. Jesus used some insights to show his interlocutor that genuine faith places man in radical dependence on God who alone, by his personal intervention, can save man. Faith, thus interpreted, means a complete upheaval in life. It supposes a "birth of the Spirit." Such a faith is necessarily faith in Christ: it depends upon recognition of his mystery. No one, except him, has "come down from heaven" (v. 13).

Is recognition to be achieved by considering the signs Jesus wrought throughout his preaching career? This was the way taken by Nicodemus, but it is a deficient way. For Saint John there can be no doubt: the place where the mystery of Jesus is unveiled is the *Cross*. This is the affirmation we find in today's verses. One must be able to see the Son of man "elevated" on the cross (v. 14) to recognize him as "elevated" in glory. The salvation of the world depends on the gift God has made to men of his only Son (vv. 16-17).

This idea of the cross being the place *par excellence* of manifestation of Christ's glory is predominant in John. It is developed most extensively in the seventeenth chapter of his gospel (Jesus' "sacerdotal prayer"). To give full value to the doctrinal content of this feast, it would have been well to refer to that.

B. DOCTRINE

A doctrinal analysis of the theme of the Cross will be found on Passion Sunday, Volume III, pp. 259-264. It will also be useful to refer the theme of Glory, Volume IV, pp. 271-278, especially p. 273.

1 November

FEAST OF ALL SAINTS

A. THE WORD

I. Revelation 7:2-4, 9-14 *1st reading*

For the author of Revelation the gathering of the servants of God before the divine throne (Rev 7) is one of the preliminaries of the "great Day."

a) A favorite concept in Revelation is that of *delay* (v. 2; cf. Rev 6:11; 11:2, 3, 7; 12:6, 14; 20:2-3). According to the description of Zechariah 6:1-7, John sees the four winds about to fall upon humanity. There is however a new factor, unforeseen by Zechariah, an order to withhold the tempest so that the elect can be assembled. The end will not come immediately. The Church must first have the opportunity to complete its mission of reassembly. This reassembly, which according to Jewish concepts was to be a sudden eschatological happening, becomes the essential task of that "delay" which constitutes the time of the Church.

b) The *reassembly* is concerned first of all with the twelve tribes (v. 4). This may seem surprising in a Christian context. We are not however dealing with convert Jews, but with the whole spiritual Israel of the Church. Thus the 144,000 are Christians simply, whether or not of Jewish origin. The saved are not an anonymous crowd, but an organized and established people. We should remember that in the time of Saint John there was no longer a division of twelve tribes in the Jewish people, though their reestablishment was part of messianic hope.

Secondly the reestablishment is concerned with the totality of nations (v. 9). The innumerable crowd should not be contrasted with the twelve tribes of the preceding verses. John is simply superimposing one image on another. The Church is seen in one as the fulfillment of the spiritual Israel, in the other as the accomplishment of salvation for the entire world. The two are superimposed in order to round off the eschatological concept. An innumerable crowd shows that the Church is truly universal, by no means a sect, a remnant, or a ghetto of separated people. The note of unity is prominent in the image of the twelve tribes. The idea of the crowd certainly comes from Daniel 3:4-7; 5:19.

All the assembled servants of God are marked on the forehead (v. 3). The mark (the image comes from Ez 9:3-6) indicates protection, salvation, a protection that comes from God himself. In this seal we can discern a symbol of the sacramental economy (cf. 2 Co 1:22; Ep 1:13; 4:30).

Verse 14 gives us a precision concerning the servants reassembled before the throne of God: "These are those who have emerged from the great trial." John is certainly thinking of the persecution of Nero, but as typical of all the trials Christians have to encounter. We should not then take the innumerable crowd as martyrs in the strict sense.

c) This *liturgy* of the Church appears as the celebration of a new feast of Tabernacles (vv. 9-10). The details mentioned (white garments, palms, acclamations, etc.) suggest the Tabernacles ritual. The feast being that of vintage and harvest was the eschatological one, that of the end of time, fulfillment. Zechariah 14:16-19 had already seen the end of time in the image of a Tabernacles feast to which all the nations would be invited (cf. also Ze 8:20 and ff.). The great prostration (vv. 11-12) is a rite of the old temple liturgy (Si 50:17-21). The adoration of God and the Lamb supersedes the adoration of the Beast.

II. 1 John 3:1-3 *2nd reading*

Verses 1 and 2 begin the second portion of John's letter. Prior to this the author has spoken principally of communion with and knowledge of God. He is now going to take up the same themes from the point of view of filiation. Verse 3 belongs to his analysis of the first condition. To live as sons of God, we must break with sin.

a) In the last verse of chapter 2 (1 Jn 2:29) there had been mention of our begetting, an image which suggests God's gift to us of his life (cf. 1 Jn 3:9; 4:7; 5:1, 4, 18). In the gospel also John had stressed the necessity of a *new birth* in baptism (Jn 3:3-8).

Begotten in this fashion, Christians can with good reason be called children of God (v. 1). The phrase however is equivocal. Many other contemporary religions claimed it for their members, including the Jewish religion itself (Dt 14:1). In such cases the phrase was metaphorical only. John insists that Christians are genuinely children of God because they share the divine life ("and that we are": v. 1). The fact of our filiation is certain, but it is still in a state of becoming. That is why the world cannot discern it. How could it, when it failed to recognize God (v. 1b)?

b) Our filiation is a reality in a state of becoming, and it is also an *eschatological reality* (v. 2). Unperceived by the world it is also sometimes unperceived by the Christian himself, whose life is often banal or difficult. He must then strive, since it is not clearly manifest now, to have it perfectly realized in the world to come. Where other religions and human techniques of divinization claim to make man equal to God by prideful means, John tells his listeners that the road which leads to divinization passes through purification (v. 3). Only the pure of heart will see God (cf. Mt 5:8; He 12:14).

III. Matthew 5:1-12a *Gospel*

The beatitudes proclaimed by Jesus were doubtless short formulas in prophetic tone which announced the advent of the Kingdom foreseen by Isaiah. In the poor, the hungry and the afflicted are discerned the beneficiaries of God's salvation (Is 58:6-10; 61:1-3; 49:8-13, etc.).

From this point of view the purpose of the beatitudes is to say that the time has come when the beneficiaries of the Kingdom will be determined not on merit or particular qualifications, but simply on the principle that God has decided to save them.

a) This prophetic tone of the beatitudes and their eschatological import Luke had used for purposes of a wisdom teaching. Those who were miserable were promised compensations here below. He interpreted the beatitudes in the light of Jesus' teaching concerning the use of riches. They are made an apologia for the social class of the poor, from which the first converts came (Ac 4:34-5:11).

Matthew's emphasis is of another order. He is concerned with a moral deepening of the gospel, and thus interprets the beatitudes in the context of the *new justice* and the spirit of the sermon on the mount. Where Luke has terms like "now" and "future," he suppresses the distinction between two moments of time. For the man who wishes to grasp it, through a life in conformity with justice, the Kingdom is already here.

b) The *poor*, who in the original rendering were the beneficiaries of God's gratuitous salvation (Is 61:1-3) become in Luke the real, sociological poor. In Matthew it is because of their spiritual, not their social, poverty that they gain the promised reward.

Where Luke regards the persecuted, the victims of events in which the Jews discerned the inauguration of the last times, as the beneficiaries of the future Kingdom, Matthew goes further by requiring that they suffer for justice' sake, not just because they are victims of a persecution. In the case of the beatitude of the hungry he makes a similar correction. Isaiah saw them as the beneficiaries of the future Kingdom (Is 49:6-13). Luke sees them as people who are really hungry for bread (see too the parable of the rich man and Lazarus). Matthew, with his moral perspective, makes them those who are hungry for justice.

To further deepen this teaching, Matthew adds four beatitudes to those of Luke. They all have the same thrust. Blessed are the "merciful" (charity and pardon), the "meek" (probably a doublet simply for "poor": the same word in Aramaic signifies both. By his doublet in translation however Matthew passes from the sociological to the spiritual meaning), the "peace-makers" (or better, the carriers of peace), and finally the "pure of heart" (a reference to the legal purity which enabled one to "see God" in the temple. For this, as in Mt 15:1-20, Matthew substitutes a more spiritual purity).

There can be no single interpretation of the beatitudes. This demonstrates that fidelity to the teaching of Jesus is something that has been lived in unanimity, but not in uniformity. Behind all of the interpretations must be an awareness of the personal intention of Jesus. In proclaiming the beatitudes he wanted to make it perfectly clear that God was really coming, and that his coming was gratuitous.

B. DOCTRINE

The Theme of Holiness

The holiness which the Church canonizes is heroic holiness. It is put forward as an example, but to most Christians it seems inimitable. Yet Jesus was addressing himself to all when he said "Be ye perfect as my heavenly father is perfect." The ideal of holiness then is not reserved for some: it is for all without exception, whatever their degree of virtue, or the standard of their moral life. They are all fundamentally in the same situation: they are sinners.

The Church's decision to institute a feast of all saints tends to reestablish in the minds of the faithful a balance that canonizable sanctity somewhat threatened. This is not a feast of saints that are canonizable by the Church. It celebrates those men and women, now deceased, who share, each according to measure, the joys of the Father's Family. The Church is reminding us that there is no essential difference between ordinary holiness and heroic holiness. In both cases holiness is the absolutely gratuitous gift God makes of his life in Jesus Christ.

This feast of all saints, with the admirable liturgical formulary that has been set for it, provides us with an opportunity of understanding more clearly the nature of the holiness we have received at baptism. Our task is to make this blossom throughout our lives.

Yahweh, the Holy One of Israel: Israel the holy people of Yahweh

As we know from the history of religions, men have always naturally tended to distinguish the "sacred" and the "profane." Man belongs to the profane world, which cannot provide him with the happiness he seeks. The sacral is a domain removed from his ordinary existence, and it is the only domain which offers the possibility of communion with the divine, where his aspirations may be crowned. This domain is cut off and can only be reached under certain conditions of ritual purity.

Isaiah was familiar with much legislation about ritual purity, which regarded the sacral as cut off from profane contact. The revelation of the God of faith however, the Totally Other, was to introduce a profound change in the erstwhile pagan legislation.

God alone is holy. Holiness is not an attribute of Yahweh: it is his very name: he is the Holy One of Israel. His absolute transcendence is defined in these terms. If there are places, persons, objects, times consecrated to Yahweh here below, that can only be by free decision of the Totally Other God. Furthermore, whatever holiness is attached to such things is radically distinct from God's holiness. There can be no question of laying hands on God by means of them.

But Yahweh wishes not only to be recognized as the one true God in a cult of which he determines the precise form. By making a covenant with Israel he decided to set her apart among nations, and to live among his people by communicating to them his holiness. Israel is a holy people: what is required from her is not a ritual holiness, but holiness of life.

Throughout all Israel's history the prophets time and again intervened to remind the chosen people of the demands laid upon them by this holiness. What is pleasing to Yahweh is a cult of obedience and love. When the people showed themselves unfaithful to the covenant, there was talk of a new covenant where the Spirit of God would guarantee their holiness, by replacing hearts of stone with a new heart.

Jesus, The Holy One filled with the Spirit

God's plan of having his creature, man, share the mystery of his own holiness, was fulfilled in the sending of the man-God. In Jesus the yearning of man for communion with the world of the divine is answered beyond all expectation. A member of the human race can be called "Holy One" as God is holy. He did not seek to exalt himself as against God: rather did he show an exemplary fidelity to the creatural condition. Filled with the Spirit, Jesus is the Holy One of God. Confronted with his miracles and his teachings, the disciples found themselves as sinful as when contrasted with God himself.

His holiness is the holiness of God's Son. This he has received [illegible]n his Father, but it is really his. It thoroughly permeates his [illegible]nity, engaging it in a constant process of sanctification. "I [illegible] myself in order that they too may be sanctified in truth" [illegible] The holiness consists in creatural love which pushes [illegible] God to the point of free acceptance of death on the [illegible] of his pilgrimage Jesus' humanity possessed the [illegible]y, and in this plenitude all human holiness

[illegible] the holy

[illegible]hrough baptism, a man is made [illegible]s-Christ and the Spirit of our [illegible]urch: "he delivered himself [illegible]her in the bath of water [illegible]. We have explicit witness to the connection between man's sanctification and the baptism of faith.

Saint Paul does not hesitate to call Christians "holy." The first letter to the Corinthians is addressed thus: "To the Church at Corinth, to those who have been sanctified in Christ Jesus, called to be saints with all who in every place invoke the name of Jesus Christ, our Lord and theirs" (1 Co 1:2; cf. also Ph 1:1). It is not a matter of exterior holiness, but of a holiness "in truth" that has been acquired by the sacrifice of Christ and is shared through faith and baptism. The source of the holiness is the action of the Holy Spirit. However, because it is in Christ Jesus that they have become holy, Christians must conform their lives to the exemplary obedience of Christ. Their ontological holiness absolutely requires their moral holiness. Their rule of conduct must be fidelity to the Beatitudes. They must act according to the holiness which comes from God, not according to carnal wisdom (2 Co 1:12).

One of the essential characteristics of holiness under the new covenant is that those made holy in Jesus Christ form an assembly. We can even say that their holiness is in proportion to their response in the context of that assembly. They are holy in other words in so far as they are members of the Church: the holines
of the Church is the primary thing. All Christians must alwa
trace their holiness to that of Christ and the Church which is
Body. The channel through which the life of the Head is c
municated. So it is that here, in assembly, we have the true vi
of Christian holiness. Christians are in assembly because the
ness of Christ is a dynamism that brings all humanity to
and that holiness is love. God, the thrice holy, is love.
that he communicates cannot be other than love.

Holiness, the prime source of missionary achievement

Mission is that act whereby the Church implants
of Christ in the spiritual quest of all peoples. It requ
sionaries leave their country, acquire the language

among whom they labor, and fashion a new visage for the Church. The accomplishment of such a task is only possible as a result of the holiness of those who undertake it. It requires total renunciation, a charity that is genuinely without limits, and a joy that is perfect.

Holiness like this makes the missionary a genuine witness to the salvation acquired in Jesus Christ: it is the very essence of salvation. Man is saved in Jesus Christ, because through him he finds the means of access to the Father's house, becomes a genuine child of God and shares God's holiness. Delivered by this means from sin, he is capable of realizing all the possibilities of the creatural state: the filial state gives an eternal dimension to the creatural one. To all this the missionary must bear witness when he proclaims Jesus Christ and the Good News of salvation.

The holy people, assembled in the Eucharist

We find the phrase "holy people" in the great eucharistic prayer. Immediately after the consecration, when the Church through the hands of the priest is offering to the Father the victim that is holy and without blemish. This becomes the name of those assembled for the Eucharist.

Here, in this celebration, the ecclesial people who share the Word and the Bread, become the holy people. Christ's holiness is communicated to them when they eat his body: the Word reverberates throughout the concrete circumstances of their lives. They are already constituted in those bonds of brotherhood which characterize in Jesus Christ the Family of the Father. Their holiness when thus assembled has an eschatological dimension.

December 8

IMMACULATE CONCEPTION OF THE VIRGIN MARY

A. THE WORD

I. Genesis 3:9-15, 20 *1st reading* This passage comes immediately after the account of the fall (Gn 3:1-6). God tries to obtain an admission of guilt, but Adam, and then Eve, attempt to excuse themselves (vv. 9-13). Then Yahweh pronounces a series of maledictions against the serpent (vv. 14-15), the woman (Gn 3:16) and the man (Gn 3:17-19). Verse 20, which is added to our reading, points out that the woman has received a name which expresses her motherhood of the human race.

a) *Sin* was regarded by Israel as a source of imbalance in the created order. Man knew that he was naked; but it was only after his fault, which was of a spiritual order, that concupiscence arose in him. The author does not contemplate a fault of the flesh: concupiscence is the consequence of the sin, and the sin consists in the loss of God's friendship.

b) The malediction against the serpent illustrates a constant principle in the Old Testament. When God punishes man, it is never an absolute punishment: there is always a possible future. In a way the account stresses the fact that God is always on the side of man. At the very moment in which he curses the serpent he opens the way to *hope*. There is at least a presentiment of salvation when Yahweh establishes enmity between the serpent and the seed of the woman. The Septuagint version will add the precision that a son of the woman will be victorious, which the Vulgate will translate as if the woman herself is destined to be victorious. Clearly however no messianic interpretation flows from the original text.

Still less does a mariological interpretation follow, something that was seen by most of the Fathers of the Church. Nevertheless there are obvious traditional reasons for the choice of this reading for the feast of the Immaculate Conception. Among the descendants of the Woman, the Virgin Mary is the one in whom God has fully restored his friendship prior to the establishment of salvation in her son, the man-God.

II. Ephesians 1:3-6, 11-12
2nd reading

Here we have extracts from the hymn of blessing (Ep 1:3-18) composed by Paul at the beginning of the letter to the Ephesians. It conforms to the classic mold of the Jewish thanksgiving. We have an introduction (v. 3), a first strophe culminating in the blessing of God (vv. 4-6), a second culminating in the glorification of God (vv. 7-12, partially missing in the reading), and finally an epiclesis where Paul begs God for knowledge of his plan for his correspondents (vv. 13-18, missing in the reading).

This thanksgiving is probably inspired by a daily thanksgiving prayer of Jewish ritual. From it would come themes like God's fatherhood (v. 3), election (v. 4), etc. An important difference between the two prayers however is that in the Jewish ritual thanks is given to God for the gift of the law, whereas in Paul's prayer the thanks is for the gift of his Son.

a) The introductory verse (v 3.) establishes at once the great themes not only of the prayer but of the entire letter. What we have is a thanksgiving for salvation (presented here as a "blessing") which is willed by the Father, merited by Christ, and realized by the Spirit.

The salutary *blessings* for which God is praised are the death and glorification of Christ (Ep 1, 7 and 10), the inauguration of divine life in man thanks to faith and baptism (Ep 1:13), and in the world thanks to Christ's Lordship (Ep 1:10). The phrase "in the heavens" which characterizes these blessings designates everything which is neither "flesh and blood" (Ep 6:12) nor the "celestial powers" supplanted by Christ (Ep 4:7-16; 5:23). The phrase "in Christ" is meant to indicate the mediation by which the blessings of the Father are conveyed. In the order of salvation Christ has been substituted for "flesh" and "spirits."

b) The first strophe (vv. 4-6) explains how God's blessing aids man, who has been called to holiness by Christ. This blessing is the *election* made by the Father's love; it transforms men into children of God. The theme of the strophe stresses God's initiative in the work of salvation and consequently the certainty of salvation itself. The object of election is holiness, communion, that is, in the very life of God (Lv 19:2). And the secret of this communion is love, a love that makes men adopted children. The verses in today's reading from the second strophe (vv. 11-12) merely reaffirm the theme of election and divine initiative.

The choice of this reading for the feast of the Immaculate Conception stresses God's portion in the mystery of Mary. She is the one chosen *par excellence* "before the creation of the world" (v. 4). And she has fully responded to this choice as the one *par excellence* who has "hoped in advance in Christ" (v. 12). God's initiative is all the more evident in that her response in hope is made with full freedom of spirit.

III. Luke 1:26-38 *Gospel*

Commentary on this gospel has been already made at the feast of the Annunciation, p. 23.

B. DOCTRINE

The Theme of Mary and the History of Salvation

The dogma of the Immaculate Conception reveals the basic role of the Virgin Mary in the human quest for salvation. That the mother of the Savior should be exempted from original sin is indeed a unique privilege, due to God's all-powerful grace. We cannot however regard this Marian dogma in terms altogether of privilege. We should be running the risk of isolating Mary from the ordinary human condition. Our understanding of salvation history would be somewhat distorted.

If, on the other hand, we regard the privilege of the Immaculate Conception, not only from the angle of God's all-powerful benevolence as he prepares in Mary a dwelling worthy of his Son, but from the standpoint of Mary herself as she freely and actively responds to God's plan, we shall be better prepared to see the light shed on mankind's spiritual adventure. Between all doctrines of the faith there is an intimate connection. Taken together they make our path clear, and give dynamism to our baptismal involvement. Isolated, they can become so much inert material, without real influence on our faith.

The Scriptures do not speak of the Immaculate Conception as such. Great theologians have shown hesitancy where the doctrine is concerned. It was only in the 19th century that the Church made a solemn proclamation. In doing so, she regarded the dogma as essential to the balance of faith as a whole, for the intimate connection of all dogmas. We are then following the path of living tradition when we try to determine how far the Immaculate Conception clarifies all salvation history.

The Immaculate Virgin, the culmination of a religion of waiting

Israel's accession to the regime of faith is an important turning point in the religious history of humanity. The religion of waiting takes definite shape. Led by the prophets, Jewish man begins to take a much more realistic view of his existence than pagan man. His insight makes him no longer content with stable and recurrent values, cosmic cycles, natural laws, the unchangeable and the predictable, all that tends to make of life a "constant recurrence" and provides security according to human measures. On the contrary he begins to estimate the event in itself, with all its dimensions of meaninglessness and unpredictability. Israel begins to see the advent of her God in the very texture of history, her own history. The encounter was extremely actual and concrete.

Her whole religious experience was a summons to deepen constantly the relationship set up by the Sinai Covenant. Yahweh is the Totally-Other God, the absolute master of his people's history. He is the only one who knows the meaning and implications of its events. He is the creator of all things, visible and invisible and need give account to no one for his actions. He leads his people: he is the Faithful One *par excellence* because he loves. Before Yahweh man is nothing, a fallible creature, but one from whom God requires an active and free response. It must be a response of the heart, engaging man's deepest being.

The discovery that God alone can save man was a realization too that the divine act was not alienating. Yahweh was seeking among men the one capable of responding in a dialogue of love. Under what conditions could man become such a partner? Because the conditions did not seem to be verified in actuality, Israel turned her gaze towards the future. She awaited the man who could give to Yahweh the "yes" of a partner. The regime of faith became a religion of Waiting.

Mary lived that religion to its ultimate implications. There was no compromise in her looking towards the future. If Yahweh was the Totally-Other, the human response also must be totally other than that within the capacity of human resources. No human state, neither membership of Israel nor observance of the law could educe it. The sort of poverty required from man was total self-renunciation and absolute openness to God's intervention. Sin had no place in Mary.

Jesus, the Savior, the son of Mary

Such was the faith of Mary that in her could be accomplished the passage from waiting to fulfillment. In such faith culminates the religious quest of humanity; it is the evil in which human salvation comes into being in the person of the man-God. We should examine what the motherhood of Mary means for an understanding of Jesus' humanity.

First of all, the Incarnation means that the Son of God took flesh from a woman among a definite people at a definite point in history. If we simply say the Word became man without further elaboration, we give the Savior's humanity an anonymity that obscures a dimension of salvation. It was not by chance that the Incarnation took place in Israel, about twelve centuries after the establishment of the chosen people, more than five centuries after the Babylonian exile. A series of prophets had enabled this people to experience more and more the pilgrimage of faith, and now the Diaspora had penetrated practically the whole known world. In so far as it is possible to measure Israel's spiritual pilgrimage, we can assert that God's Son intervened in history at the moment most suited to his mission.

What we know of Mary enables us to penetrate deeper into the mystery of Christ. When she bore the Messiah, she did not just give him a body. She was his mother in the full sense of the term. In other words the Son of God fitted into Israel's spiritual pilgrimage as one who had been already modeled by a living tradition. From his mother he derived the treasures of faith accumulated by generations of believers in Israel. He was deeply educated in the faith of his fathers.

Then, because of the Immaculate Conception, the motherhood of Mary had a unique dimension. Sinless as she was, she had lived the religion of waiting in that spiritual poverty which would be that of her Son in the religion of fulfillment. By transmitting to Jesus that which was best in her she was really preparing him for the way of obedience unto the death of the cross.

In the Incarnation of his Son God showed infinite respect for the spiritual quest of humanity. At the human level the Son received everything from Mary; and because he was the eternal Son of the Father he brought the gift of eternal life. What the dogma of the Immaculate Conception reveals is the extent to which the Savior himself espoused the human spiritual quest.

The motherhood of Mary and the Church

Mary's immaculate motherhood also enables us to penetrate the mystery of the Church. She was its first believer. For all its exceptional quality the faith of Mary depended on Christ alone for its salvific value, and the same is true of the faith of the Church. Yet, from another angle, the very quality of her faith shows the extent to which man is summoned to contribute in the realization of the salvific plan. And the same is true of the faith of the Church. The Church is the body of Christ, but she is also his Spouse, bringing her unique and irreplaceable stone for the building of salvation.

In order to safeguard the absolute transcendence of Christ's being and action, a tendency could develop whereby the Church would be considered as merely some sort of "extension" of the Risen Lord. She would be merely an instrument of the glorified Christ. Here the motherhood of Mary is a corrective. The Church is indeed the Body of Christ, but this Body gets its "materials" so to speak from the concrete individuals who form it. Just as Mary gave birth to the body of the Son of God, the Church throughout its history continues to bring forth the Body of Christ.

The fact that this is so is sufficient evidence of the extraordinary responsibility of the Christian in salvation-history. It is the context in which we must estimate the greatness as well as the weakness in Christian history. Priests or lay persons, popes or princes, have in the past made options which opened the way for new action by the Spirit, or on the other hand impeded such action. When we learn for instance that the Jesuit missionary enterprise in China in the 17th and 18th centuries brought the emperor to the brink of conversion, and that he stopped short because of the contrary factors he could not help observing, we realize that here was a moment when another decision might have had incalculable consequences for the history of the Church and of humanity.

In line with the dogmatic constitution on the Church, promulgated by the second Vatican Council, we must once more emphasize the fact that baptism enables a man to intervene with efficacy in human history. Too often people take too narrow a view of baptism, as if it were the gateway to individual salvation only. The truth is that it begets responsibilities that have to do with the salvation of all. If we are members of the Body of Christ, we are each shaping the image of her whose mission is one of manifesting the salvation acquired once for all in Jesus Christ. We are determining the path she takes.

The mystery of Mary and the future of humanity

Tradition has often dwelt on the role of Mary in what might be termed "providential preparations" for salvation in Jesus Christ. Belonging to the Israelite tradition, she had the last word in the religion of waiting. In her the religious quest of her people reached completion. Because she has passed that way herself, she knows better than any other the path to be followed in order to reach the gift of God. Being the mother of the Son of God, she realizes the close connection between the religion of waiting and that of fulfillment. When the Son of God takes flesh, all is radically changed. Where, prior to this we had the pre-history of salvation, now begins its history. Between history and prehistory however there is a close continuity.

This very role that she played in Israel's history, she secretly plays in all salvation history. In order that the mystery of Christ be incarnated in the spiritual itinerary of any people or any culture, a long period of waiting will be necessary. The mystery of Christ is not something imported, it must be gradually engrafted. During this time of slow maturation Mary will be present. She knows the search of this pilgrimage which culminates in welcome from the Lord. New bringings to birth of the Word are her province. Thanks to the communion of saints she can play a determining role in leading the nations to the proper path.

Thus in all missionary spirituality contemplation of the mystery of Mary is essential. What she is to the nations on the other side of death, the missionary must try to be here below. He must be Greek with the Greeks, Indian with the Indians, Chinese with the Chinese. He must not bring the Good News as it were from the outside. He must share the language of a new people, share the most secret nuances of their quest, make his own their questionings and their aspirations. All his efforts must be directed so that this people can contribute to the building of the human future.

Today world mission is characterized by the dialogue between Christian and non-Christian religions. The idea has been familiar for some years, but it will be a considerable time before all its possibilities can be plumbed. In concrete terms dialogue for the missionary will mean sharing the other's pilgrimage, making the quest his too. It is a course on which he was preceded by the Virgin Mary.

Eucharistic celebration and salvation history

The feast of the Immaculate Conception has its established place in a liturgy concerned with the future of humanity. Those who celebrate it have an excellent opportunity of gaining deeper insight into what is meant by participation in the Eucharist.

The Eucharist is an act of Christ and would have no value without him. But it is also the act of a definite ecclesial community, and in this sense is stamped with the image of the assembled members. One does not participate in it merely to receive; each member is summoned to an active part in the great rite. All that we have already said concerning the mystery of the Church, in the light of the mystery of Mary, is especially valid at this eucharistic moment. The "yes" pronounced there by all the members is symbolic of the actual Church and consequently of human destiny too. All Christians assembled in this rite should have a keen awareness of what is happening. The closest link we have with the living Christ is this sharing of the bread and the word, and the "yes" that should accompany it engages the members of Christ's Body at the deepest level of their being.

Nor do we ever come alone to the Eucharist. We come as representatives, representing our natural communities, our people, our cultural ambience. We are part of a collective future, the goal of the quest that is carried out in all these groups. All takes place so that Christ can go on being born "until the day that he returns."

SECOND PART

The New Lectionary. Indexes indicating references to the commentaries in the Guides

I. THE SUNDAY LECTIONARY

First Sunday of Advent

A. Is 2:1-5 — I, 1
Rm 13:11-14 — I, 6
Mt 24:37-44 — I, 10

B. Is 63:16b-17; 64:1, 4-8ab — I, 3
1 Co 1:3-9 — I, 8
Mk 13:33-37 — I, 12

C. Jr 33:14-16 — I, 5
I Th 3:12-4:2 — I, 9
Lk 21:25-28, 34-36 — I, 13

Second Sunday of Advent

A. Is 11:1-10 — I, 47
Rm 15:4-9 — I, 53
Mt 3:1-12 — I, 59

B. Is 40:1-5, 9-11 — I, 49
2 P 3:8-14 — I, 54
Mk 1:1-8 — I, 63

C. Ba 5:1-9 — I, 51
Ph 1:4-6 & 8-11 — I, 58
Lk 3:1-6 — I, 65

Third Sunday of Advent

A. Is 35:1-6a, 10 — I, 91
Jm 5:7-10 — I, 93
Mt 11:2-11 — I, 97

B. Is 61:1-2, 10-11 — I, 91
1 Th 5:16-24 — I, 94
Jn 1:6-8; 19-28 — I, 99

C. Zp 3:14-18a — I, 92
Ph 4:4-7 — I, 95
Lk 3:10-18 — I, 100

Fourth Sunday of Advent

A. Is 7:10-14 — I, 130
Rm 1:1-7 — I, 135
Mt 1:18-24 — I, 140

B. 2 S 7:1-5, 8b-11, 16 — I, 131
Rm 16:25-27 — I, 137
Lk 1:26-38 — I, 142

C. Mi 5:2-5a — I, 134
Heb 10:5-10 — I, 138
Lk 1:39-45 — I, 146

Eve and Feast of Christmas

Christmas Eve:
Is 62:1-5 — I, 177
Mt 1:1-25 — I, 178

Midnight:
Is 9:1-7 — I, 178
Tt 2:11-14 — I, 183
Lk 2:1-14 — I, 187

Dawn:
Is 62:11-12 — I, 180
Tt 3:4-7 — I, 183
Lk 2:15-20 — I, 187

Day:
Is 52:7-10 — I, 181
Heb 1:1-6 — I, 185
Jn 1:1-18 — I, 189

Sunday Within the Octave of Christmas

A. Si 3:3-7, 14-17a — I, 203
Col 3:12-21 — I, 204
Mt 2:13-14, 19-23 — I, 206

B. Si 3:3-7, 14-17a — I, 203
Col 3:12-21 — I, 204
Lk 2:22, 39-40 — I, 208

C. Si 3:3-7, 14-17a — I, 203
Col 3:12-21 — I, 204
Lk 2:41-52 — I, 209

Octave of Christmas

Nb 6:22-27	I, 241
Ga 4:4-7	I, 241
Lk 2:16-21	I, 244

Feast of the Epiphany

Is 60:1-6	I, 252
Ep 3:2-3a, 5-6	I, 253
Mt 2:1-12	I, 254

First Sunday—
Baptism of Jesus

A. Is 42:1-4, 6-7	I, 301
Ac 10:34-38	I, 302
Mt 3:13-17	I, 304
B. Is 42:1-4, 6-7	I, 301
Ac 10:34-38	I, 302
Mk 1:7-11	I, 307
C. Is 42:1-4, 6-7	I, 301
Ac 10:34-38	I, 302
Lk 3:15-18, 21-22	I, 307

First Sunday of Lent

A. Gn 2:7-9; 3:1-7	III, 9
Rm 5:12-19	III, 12
Mt 4:1-11	III, 20
B. Gn 9:8-15	III, 10
1 P 3:18-22	III, 16
Mk 1:12-15	III, 21
C. Dt 26:4-10	III, 11
Rm 10:8-13	III, 19
Lk 4:1-13	III, 23

Second Sunday of Lent

A. Gn 12:1-17	III, 62
2 Tm 1:8b-10	III, 68
Mt 17:1-9	III, 72
B. Gn 22:1-2, 9a, 10-13, 15-18	III, 64
Rm 8:31b-34	III, 69
Mk 9:2-9	III, 75
C. Gn 15:5-12, 17-18	III, 66
Ph 3:17-4:1	III, 71
Lk 9:28b-36	III, 77

Third Sunday of Lent

A. Ex 24:12, 15-18	III, 110
Rm 5:1-2, 5-8	III, 117
Jn 4:5-42	III, 123
B. Ex 20:1-17	III, 111
1 Co 1:22-25	III, 119
Jn 2:13-25	III, 127
C. Ex 3:1-8a, 13-15	III, 115
1 Co 10:1-6, 10-12	III, 121
Lk 13:1-9	III, 129

Fourth Sunday of Lent

A. 1 S 16:1b, 6-7, 10-13a	III, 164
Ep 5:8-14	III, 167
Jn 9:1-41	III, 171
B. 2 Ch 36:14-16, 19-23	III, 165
Ep 2:4-10	III, 168
Jn 3:14-21	III, 175
C. Jos 5:9a, 10-12	III, 166
2 Co 5:17-21	III, 169
Lk 15:1-3, 11-32	III, 177

Fifth Sunday of Lent

A. Ez 37:12-14	III, 207
Rm 8:8-11	III, 211
Jn 11:1-45	III, 215
B. Jr 31:31-34	III, 208
Heb 5:7-10	III, 211
Jn 12:20-33	III, 217
C. Is 43:16-21	III, 210
Ph 3:8-14	III, 212
Jn 8:1-11	III, 231

Passion Sunday

Blessing:

A. Mt 21:1-11	III, 249
B. Mk 11:1-10	—
C. Lk 19, 28-40	—

Masses:

A. Is 50, 4-7	III, 250
Ph 2:6-11	III, 250
Mt 26:14-27:66	III, 253
B. Is 50, 4-7	III, 250
Ph 2:6-11	III, 250
Mk 14:1-15:47	III, 255
C. Is 50, 4-7	III, 250
Ph 2:6-11	III, 250
Lk 22:39-23:56	III, 257

Mass of the Chrism

Is 61:1-3a, 8b-9	III, 280
Rv 1:5-8	III, 281
Lk 4:16-21	III, 283

Mass Holy Thursday

Ex 12:1-8, 11-14	III, 285
1 Co 11:23-26	III, 288
Jn 13:1-15	III, 290

Good Friday

Is 52:13-53:12	III, 293
Heb 4:14-16; 5:7-9	III, 294
Jn 18:1-19, 42	III, 296

EASTER

Vigil Readings:

1. Gn 1:1-2:2	III, 318
2. Gn 22:1-18	III, 319
3. Ex 14:15-15:1	III, 319
4. Is 54:1-11	III, 321
5. Is 55:1-11	III, 322
6. Ba 3:9-15, 32; 4:4	III, 324
7. Ez 36:16-28	VI, 296

Vigil Epistle:

Rm 6:3-11	III, 325

Vigil Gospels:

Mt 28:1-10	III, 328
Mk 16:1-8	III, 329
Lk 24:1-12	III, 330

Easter Readings:

1. Ac 10:34a, 37-43	III, 331
2. Col 3:1-4	III, 332
3. Jn 20:1-9	III, 334

Evening Easter Reading:

Lk 24:13-35	III, 336

Second Sunday of Easter

A. Ac 2:42-47	IV, 22
1 P 1:3-9	IV, 25
Jn 20:19-31	IV, 30
B. Ac 4:32-35	IV, 22
1 Jn 5:1-6	IV, 28
Jn 20:19-31	IV, 30
C. Ac 5:12-16	IV, 22
Rv 1:9-13, 17-19	IV, 29
Jn 20:19-31	IV, 30

Third Sunday of Easter

A. Ac 2:14, 22-28	IV, 61
1 P 1:17-21	IV, 71
Lk 24:13-35	IV, 78
B. Ac 3:13-15, 17-19	IV, 66
1 Jn 2:1-5	IV, 73
Lk 24:35-48	IV, 79
C. Ac 5:27-32, 40-41	IV, 68
Rv 5:11-14	IV, 75
Jn 21:1-19	IV, 81

Fourth Sunday of Easter

A. Ac 2:14, 36-41	IV, 113
1 P 2:20-25	IV, 116
Jn 10:1-10	IV, 121
B. Ac 4:8-12	IV, 114
1 Jn 3:1-2	IV, 118
Jn 10:11-18	IV, 123
C. Ac 13:14, 43-52	IV, 114
Rv 7:9, 14-17	IV, 119
Jn 10:27-30	IV, 125

Fifth Sunday of Easter

A.	Ac 6:1-7	IV, 154
	1 P 2:4-9	IV, 159
	Jn 14:1-12	IV, 166
B.	Ac 9:26-31	IV, 156
	1 Jn 3:18-24	IV, 161
	Jn 15:1-8	IV, 168
C.	Ac 14:21-27	IV, 157
	Rv 21:1-5	IV, 162
	Jn 13:31-35	IV, 169

Sixth Sunday of Easter

A.	Ac 8:5-8; 14-17	IV, 195
	1 P 3:15-18	IV, 198
	Jn 14:15-21	IV, 201
B.	Ac 10:25-26, 34-35, 44-48	IV, 196
	1 Jn 4:7-10	IV, 199
	Jn 15:9-17	IV, 203
C.	Ac 15:1-2, 22-29	IV, 197
	Rv 21:10-14, 22-23	IV, 200
	Jn 14:23-29	IV, 204

Ascension

A.	Ac 1:1-11	IV, 228
	Ep 1:17-23	IV, 230
	Mt 28:16-20	IV, 232
B.	Ac 1:1-11	IV, 228
	Ep 1:17-23	IV, 230
	Mk 16:15-20	IV, 234
C.	Ac 1:1-11	IV, 228
	Ep 1:17-23	IV, 230
	Lk 24:46-53	IV, 238

Seventh Sunday of Easter

A.	Ac 1:12-14	IV, 251
	1 P 4:13-16	IV, 256
	Jn 17:1-11	IV, 259
B.	Ac 1:15-17, 20-26	IV, 252
	1 Jn 4:11-16	IV, 257
	Jn 17:11b-19	IV, 261
C.	Ac 7:55-60	IV, 254
	Rv 22:12-14, 16-17, 20	IV, 258
	Jn 17:20-26	IV, 263

Pentecost

Vigil:

Ez 36:25-28	IV, 291
or Gn 11:1-9	II, 278
or Ex 19:3-8a, 16-20b	VI, 200
or Ez 37:1-14	VI, 302
or Jl 3:1-5	—
Rm 8:22-27	IV, 292
Jn 7:37-39	IV, 294

Feast:

Ac 2:1-11	IV, 295
1 Co 12:3b-7, 12-13	IV, 299
Jn 20:19-23	IV, 301

Feast of the Trinity

A.	Ex 34:4-6, 8-9	IV, 314
	2 Co 13:11-13	IV, 318
	Jn 3:16-18	IV, 324
B.	Dt 4:32-34, 39-40	IV, 315
	Rm 8:14-17	IV, 319
	Mt 28:16-20	IV, 326
C.	Pr 8:22-31	IV, 316
	Rm 5:1-5	IV, 321
	Jn 16:12-15	IV, 326

Feast of Corpus Christi

A.	Dt 8:2-3, 14-16	IV, 335
	1 Co 10:16-17	IV, 339
	Jn 6:51-58	IV, 344
B.	Ex 24:3-8	IV, 336
	Heb 9:11-15	IV, 340
	Mk 14:12-16, 22-26	IV, 345
C.	Gn 14:18-20	IV, 337
	1 Co 11:23-26	IV, 342
	Lk 9:11-17	IV, 346

Feast of the Sacred Heart

A.	Dt 7:6-11	IV, 358
	1 Jn 4:7-16	IV, 362
	Mt 11:25-30	IV, 366
B.	Ho 11:1, 3-4, 8-9	IV, 359
	Ep 3:8-12, 14-19	IV, 362
	Jn 19:31-37	IV, 369
C.	Ez 34:11-16	IV, 360
	Rm 5:5-11	IV, 364
	Lk 15:3-7	IV, 371

Second Sunday

A.	Is 49:3, 5-6	II, 21
	1 Co 1:1-3	II, 24
	Jn 1:29-34	II, 29
B.	1 S 3:3b-10, 19	II, 22
	1 Co 6:13-15, 17-20	II, 25
	Jn 1:35-42	II, 32
C.	Is 62:1-5	II, 23
	1 Co 12:4-11	II, 27
	Jn 2:1-12	II, 34

Third Sunday

A.	Is 9:1-4	II, 73
	1 Co 1:10-13, 17	II, 76
	Mt 4:12-23	II, 80
B.	Jon 3:1-5, 10	II, 74
	1 Co 7:29-31	II, 78
	Mk 1:14-20	II, 83
C.	Neh 8:1-4a, 5-6, 8-10	II, 76
	1 Co 12:12-30	II, 79
	Lk 1:1-4; 4:14-21	II, 85

Fourth Sunday

A.	Zp 2:3; 3:12-13	II, 128
	1 Co 1:26-31	II, 131
	Mt 5:1-12a	II, 137
B.	Dt 18:15-20	II, 129
	1 Co 7:32-35	II, 133
	Mk 1:21-28	II, 140
C.	Jr 1:4-5, 17-19	II, 130
	1 Co 12:31-13:13	II, 135
	Lk 4:21-30	II, 141

Fifth Sunday

A.	Is 58:7-10	II, 177
	1 Co 2:1-5	II, 180
	Mt 5:13-16	II, 185
B.	Jb 7:1-4, 6-7	II, 178
	1 Co 9:16-19, 22-23	II, 181
	Mk 1:29-39	II, 186
C.	Is 6:1-2a, 3-8	II, 178
	1 Co 15:1-11	II, 183
	Lk 5:1-11	II, 188

Sixth Sunday

A.	Si 15:16-21	II, 237
	1 Co 2:6-10	II, 239
	Mt 5:17-37	II, 242
B.	Lv 13:1-2, 45-46	II, 238
	1 Co 10:31-11:1	II, 240
	Mk 1:40-45	II, 246
C.	Jr 17:5-8	II, 238
	1 Co 15:12, 16-20	II, 241
	Lk 6:17, 20-26	II, 248

Seventh Sunday

A.	Lv 19:1-2, 17-18	II, 288
	1 Co 3:16-23	II, 292
	Mt 5:38-48	II, 296
B.	Is 43:18-19, 21-22, 24b-25	II, 290
	2 Co 1:18-22	II, 293
	Mk 2:1-12	II, 298
C.	1 S 26:2, 7-9, 12-13, 22-23	II, 291
	1 Co 15:45-49	II, 295
	Lk 6:27-38	II, 300

Eighth Sunday

A.	Is 49:14-15	II, 328
	1 Co 4:1-5	II, 331
	Mt 6:24-34	II, 335
B.	Ho 2:16-17, 21-22	II, 329
	2 Co 3:17-4:2	II, 332
	Mk 2:18-22	II, 338
C.	Si 27:5-8	II, 330
	1 Co 15:54-58	II, 334
	Lk 6:39-45	II, 339

Ninth Sunday

A.	Dt 11:18, 26-28	V, 1
	Rm 3:21-25, 28	V, 5
	Mt 7:21-27	V, 11
B.	Dt 5:12-15	V, 2
	2 Co 4:6-11	V, 7
	Mk 2:23-3:6	V, 13
C.	1 K 8:41-43	V, 4
	Ga 1:1-2, 6-10	V, 9
	Lk 7:1-10	V, 15

Tenth Sunday

A.	Ho 6:3-6	V, 32
	Rm 4:18-25	V, 35
	Mt 9:9-13	V, 40
B.	Gn 3:9-15	V, 32
	2 Co 4:13-5:1	V, 37
	Mk 3:20-35	V, 41
C.	1 K 17:17-24	V, 34
	Ga 1:11-19	V, 38
	Lk 7:11-17	V, 43

Eleventh Sunday

A.	Ex 19:2-6	V, 57
	Rm 5:6-11	V, 62
	Mt 9:36-10:8	V, 65
B.	Ez 17:22-24	V, 58
	2 Co 5:6-10	V, 63
	Mk 4:26-34	V, 68
C.	2 S 12:7-10, 13	V, 60
	Ga 2:16, 19:21	V, 64
	Lk 7:36-50	V, 69

Twelfth Sunday

A.	Jr 20:10-13	V, 83
	Rm 5:12-15	V, 87
	Mt 10:26-33	V, 95
B.	Jb 38:1, 8-11	V, 85
	2 Co 5:14-17	V, 92
	Mk 4:35-41	V, 97
C.	Zc 12:10-11	V, 86
	Ga 3:26-29	V, 93
	Lk 9:18-24	V, 98

Thirteenth Sunday

A.	2 K 4:8-11, 14-16	V, 111
	Rm 6:3-4, 8-11	V, 114
	Mt 10:37-42	V, 120
B.	Ws 1:13-15; 2:23-24	V, 111
	2 Co 8:7-9, 13-15	V, 116
	Mk 5:21-43	V, 121
C.	1 K 19:16, 19-21	V, 112
	Ga 5:1, 13-18	V, 118
	Lk 9:51-62	V, 123

Fourteenth Sunday

A.	Zc 9:9-10	V, 141
	Rm 8:9, 11-13	V, 143
	Mt 11:25-30	V, 147
B.	Ez 2:2-5	V, 142
	2 Co 12:7-10	V, 144
	Mk 6:1-6	V, 150
C.	Is 66:10-14	V, 142
	Ga 6:14-18	V, 145
	Lk 10:1-12, 17-20	V, 151

Fifteenth Sunday

A.	Is 55:10-11	V, 166
	Rm 8:18-23	V, 169
	Mt 13:1-23	V, 176

B. Am 7:12-15	V, 167
Ep 1:3-14	V, 170
Mk 6:7-13	V, 177
C. Dt 30:10-14	V, 168
Col 1:15-20	V, 173
Lk 10:25-37	V, 177

Sixteenth Sunday

A. Ws 12:13, 16-19	V, 192
Rm 8:26-27	V, 196
Mt 13:24-30, 36-43	V, 200
B. Jr 23:1-6	V, 193
Ep 2:13-18	V, 198
Mk 6:30-34	V, 202
C. Gn 18:1-10	V, 194
Col 1:24-28	V, 199
Lk 10:38-42	V, 203

Seventeenth Sunday

A. 1 K 3:5, 7-12	V, 217
Rm 8:28-30	V, 220
Mt 13:44-52	V, 224
B. 2 K 4:42-44	V, 217
Ep 4:1-6	V, 221
Jn 6:1-15	V, 227
C. Gn 18:20-33	V, 218
Col 2:12-14	V, 223
Lk 11:1-13	V, 229

Eighteenth Sunday

A. Is 55:1-3	V, 245
Rm 8:35, 37-39	V, 248
Mt 14:13-21	V, 253
B. Ex 16:2-4, 12-15	V, 246
Ep 4:17, 20-24	V, 250
Jn 6:24-35	V, 254
C. Ecc 1:2; 2:21-23	V, 247
Col 3:1-5, 9-11	V, 251
Lk 12:13-21	V, 256

Nineteenth Sunday

A. 1 K 19:9, 11-13	V, 268
Rm 9:1-5	V, 271
Mt 14:22-33	V, 276
B. 1 K 19:4-8	V, 269
Ep 4:30-5:2	V, 273
Jn 6:41-51	V, 278
C. Ws 18:6-9	V, 270
Heb 11:1-2, 8-12	V, 275
Lk 12:31-38	V, 280

Twentieth Sunday

A. Is 56:1, 6-7	V, 296
Rm 11:13-15, 29-32	V, 299
Mt 15:21-28	V, 303
B. Pr 9:1-6	V, 297
Ep 5:15-20	V, 300
Jn 6:51-59	V, 304
C. Jr 38:4-6, 8-10	V, 298
Heb 12:1-4	V, 302
Lk 12:49-53	V, 306

Twenty-First Sunday

A. Is 22:19-23	V, 321
Rm 11:33-36	V, 325
Mt 16:13-20	V, 329
B. Jos 24:1-2, 15-17, 18b	V, 321
Ep 5:21-32	V, 326
Jn 6:61-70	V, 331
C. Is 66:18-21	V, 323
Heb 12:5-7, 11-13	V, 328
Lk 13:21-30	V, 332

Twenty-Second Sunday

A. Jr 20:7-9	VII, 1
Rm 12:1-2	VII, 4
Mt 16:21-27	VII, 10
B. Dt 4:1-2, 6-8	VII, 2
Jm 1:17-18, 21b-22, 27	VII, 6
Mk 7:1-8, 14-15, 21-23	VII, 13

Thirtieth Sunday

A. Ex 22:20-26	VII, 206
1 Th 1:5-10	VII, 208
Mt 22:34-40	VII, 210
B. Jr 31:7-9	VII, 206
Heb 5:1-6	VII, 209
Mk 10:46-52	VII, 211
C. Si 35:12-14, 16-18	VII, 207
2 Tm 4:6-8, 16-18	VII, 209
Lk 18:9-14	VII, 213

Thirty-First Sunday

A. Ml 1:14-2:2, 8-10	VII, 227
1 Th 2:7-9, 13	VII, 230
Mt 23:1-12	VII, 232
B. Dt 6:2-6	VII, 228
Heb 7:23-28	VII, 231
Mk 12:28-34	VII, 234
C. Ws 11:23-12:1	VII, 229
2 Th 1:11-2:2	VII, 232
Lk 19:1-10	VII, 235

Thirty-Second Sunday

A. Ws 6:12-16	VII, 249
1 Th 4:13-18	VII, 252
Mt 25:1-13	VII, 255
B. 1 K 17:10-16	VII, 249
Heb 9:24-28	VII, 253
Mk 12:38-44	VII, 257
C. 2 M 7:1-2, 9-14	VII, 250
2 Th 2:16-3:5	VII, 254
Lk 20:27-38	VII, 258

Thirty-Third Sunday

A. Pr 31:10-13, 19-20, 30-31	VII, 273
1 Th 5:1-6	VII, 275
Mt 25:14-30	VII, 278
B. Dn 12:1-3	VII, 273
Heb 10:11-14, 18	VII, 276
Mk 13:24-32	VII, 280
C. Ml 3:19-20	VII, 274
2 Th 3:7-12	VII, 277
Lk 21:5-19	VII, 282

Thirty-Fourth Sunday
(Feast of Christ the King)

A. Ez 34:11-12, 15-17	VII, 295
1 Co 15:20-26, 28	VII, 299
Mt 25:31-46	VII, 303
B. Dn 7:13-14	VII, 296
Rv 1:5-8	VII, 300
Jn 18:33-37	VII, 306
C. 2 S 5:1-3	VII, 298
Col 1:12-20	VII, 301
Lk 23:35-43	VII, 307

II. THE WEEKDAY LECTIONARY

First Week of Advent

	1st reading		*Gospel*	
Monday	Is 4:2-6*	I, 28	Mt 8:5-11	I, 29
Tuesday	Is 11:1-10	I, 31	Lk 10:21-24	I, 32
Wednesday	Is 25:6-10a	I, 34	Mt 15:29-37	I, 36
Thursday	Is 26:1-6	I, 37	Mt 7:21, 24-27	I, 39
Friday	Is 29:17-24	I, 41	Mt 9:27-31	I, 42
Saturday	Is 30:19-21, 23-26	I, 43	Mt 9:35 & 10:1, 6-8	I, 44

Second Week of Advent

Monday	Is 35:1-10	I, 78	Lk 5:17-26	I, 78
Tuesday	Is 40:1-10	I, 80	Mt 18:12-14	I, 80
Wednesday	Is 40:25-31	I, 82	Mt 11:28-30	I, 83
Thursday	Is 41:13-20	I, 85	Mt 11:11-15	I, 86
Friday	Is 48:17-19	I, 87	Mt 11:16-19	I, 87
Saturday	Si 48:1-4, 9-11	I, 88	Mt 17:10-13	I, 90

Third Week of Advent

Monday	Nb 24:2-7, 15-17	I, 115	Mt 21:23-27	I, 116
Tuesday	Zp 3:1-2, 9-13	I, 117	Mt 21:28-32	I, 119
Wednesday	Is 45:6b-8; 18:21b-25	I, 120	Lk 7:19-23	I, 121
Thursday	Is 54:1-10	I, 123	Lk 7:24-30	I, 124
Friday	Is 56:1-3a, 6-8	I, 126	Jn 5:33-36	I, 127

Last Days Before Christmas

December 17	Gn 49:2, 8-10	I, 160	Mt 1:1-17	I, 160
December 18	Jr 23:5-8	I, 162	Mt 1:18-24	I, 163
December 19	Jg 13:2-7; 24-25a	I, 163	Lk 1:5-25	I, 164
December 20	Is 7:10-14	I, 166	Lk 1:26-38	I, 166
December 21	Ct 2:8-14	I, 166	Lk 1:39-45	I, 167
December 22	1 S 1:24-28	I, 168	Lk 1:46-56	I, 168
December 23	Ml 3:1-4; 4:5-6	I, 170	Lk 1:57-66	I, 172
December 24	2 S 7:1-5, 8b-11, 16	I, 173	Lk 1:67-79	I, 175

Octave of Christmas

December 26	Ac 6:8-10 & 7:54-69	I, 222	Mt 10:17-22	I, 224
December 27	1 Jn 1:1-4	I, 225	Jn 20:2-8	I, 227
December 28	1 Jn 1:5-2:2	I, 228	Mt 2:13-18	I, 231
December 29	1 Jn 2:3-11	I, 231	Lk 2:22-35	I, 233

*See first Sunday of Advent for commentary Is 2:1-5, Vol. I, p. 21.

	1st reading		*Gospel*	
December 30	1 Jn 2:12-17	I, 236	Lk 2:36-40	I, 237
December 31	1 Jn 2:18-21	I, 239	Jn 1:1-18	I, 240

First Days of the Year

January 2	1 Jn 2:22-28	I, 269	Jn 1:19-28	I, 269
January 3	1 Jn 2:29-3:6	I, 270	Jn 1:29-34	I, 271
January 4	1 Jn 3:7-10	I, 273	Jn 1:35-42	I, 273
January 5	1 Jn 3:11-21	I, 275	Jn 1:43-51	I, 277
January 6	Si 24:1-4, 12-16	I, 278	Jn 1:1-18	I, 281
January 7	1 Jn 3:22-4, 6	I, 281	Mt 4:12-17, 23-25	I, 283
January 8	1 Jn 4:7-10	I, 284	Mk 6:34-44	I, 284
January 9	1 Jn 4:11-18	I, 287	Mk 6:45-52	I, 289
January 10	1 Jn 4:19-5:4	I, 290	Lk 4:14-22	I, 291
January 11	1 Jn 5:5-13	I, 294	Lk 5:12-16	I, 296
January 12	1 Jn 5:14-21	I, 297	Jn 3:22-30	I, 299

* * *

Week of Ash Wednesday

Wednesday	Jl 2:12-18	III, 1	Mt 6:1-6, 16-18	III, 1
Thursday	Dt 30:15-20	III, 3	Lk 9:22-25	III, 3
Friday	Is 58:1-9a	III, 4	Mt 9:14-15	III, 6
Saturday	Is 58:9b-14	III, 4	Lk 5:27-32	III, 7

First Week of Lent

Monday	Lv 19:1-2, 11-18	III, 39	Mt 25:31-46	III, 41
Tuesday	Is 55:10-11	III, 44	Mt 6:7-15	III, 44
Wednesday	Jon 3:1-10	III, 47	Mt 12:38-42	III, 49
Thursday	Est 14:1-5, 12-14	III, 51	Mt 7:7-12	III, 52
Friday	Ez 18:21-28	III, 54	Mt 5:20-26	III, 54
Saturday	Dt 26:16-19	III, 57	Mt 5:43-48	III, 59

Second Week of Lent

Monday	Dn 9:4b-10	III, 89	Lk 6:36-38	III, 89
Tuesday	Is 1:10, 16-20	III, 98	Mt 23:1-12	III, 95
Wednesday	Jr 18:18-20	III, 97	Mt 20:17-28	III, 98
Thursday	Jr 17:5-10	III, 101	Lk 16:19-31	III, 102
Friday	Gn 37:3-4, 12-13a, 17b-28	III, 104	Mt 21:33-43, 45-46	III, 105
Saturday	Mi 7:14-15, 18-20	III, 108	Lk 15:1-3, 11-32	III, 109

Third Week of Lent

Monday	2 K 5:1-15a	III, 143	Lk 4:24-30	III, 144
Tuesday	Dn 3:25, 34-43	III, 146	Mt 18:21-35	III, 148
Wednesday	Dt 4:1, 5-9	III, 151	Mt 5:17-19	III, 152

	1st reading			*Gospel*	
Thursday	Jr 7:23-28	III, 153		Lk 11:14-23	III, 155
Friday	Ho 14:2-10	III, 156		Mk 12:28b-34	III, 158
Saturday	Ho 6:1-6	III, 160		Lk 18:9-14	III, 161
Fourth Week of Lent					
Monday	Is 65:17-21	III, 190		Jn 4:43-54	III, 191
Tuesday	Ez 47:1-9, 12	III, 193		Jn 5:1-3, 5-16	III, 194
Wednesday	Is 49:8-15	III, 196		Jn 5:17-30	III, 197
Thursday	Ex 32:7-14	III, 199		Jn 5:31-47	III, 200
Friday	Ws 2:1a, 12-22	III, 201		Jn 7:1-2, 25-30	III, 202
Saturday	Jr 11:18-20	III, 203		Jn 7:40-53	III, 205
Fifth Week of Lent					
Monday	Dn 13:1-9; 15-17;			Jn 8:1-11	III, 231
	19-30; 33-62	III, 231	Alt	Jn 8:12-20	III, 233
Tuesday	Nb 21:4-9	III, 235		Jn 8:21-30	III, 236
Wednesday	Dn 3:14-20, 91-92,			Jn 8:31-42	III, 238
	95	III, 237			
Thursday	Gn 17:3-9	III, 241		Jn 8:51-59	III, 243
Friday	Jr 20:10-13	III, 244		Jn 10:31-42	III, 245
Saturday	Ez 37:21-28	III, 245		Jn 11:45-57	III, 246
Holy Week					
Monday	Is 42:1-7	III, 270		Jn 12:1-11	III, 271
Tuesday	Is 49:1-6	III, 272		Jn 13:21-33, 36-38	III, 274
Wednesday	Is 50:4-9a	III, 275		Mt 26:14-25	III, 278
Octave of Easter					
Monday	Ac 2:14, 22-32	IV, 1		Mt 28:8-15	IV, 1
Tuesday	Ac 2:36-41	IV, 2		Jn 20:11-18	IV, 2
Wednesday	Ac 3:1-10	IV, 4		Lk 24:13-35	IV, 6
Thursday	Ac 3:11-26	IV, 9		Lk 24:35-48	IV, 11
Friday	Ac 4:1-12	IV, 11		Jn 21:1-14	IV, 13
Saturday	Ac 4:13-21	IV, 17		Mk 16:9-15	IV, 17
Second Week of Easter					
Monday	Ac 4:23-31	IV, 48		Jn 3:1-15	IV, 50
Tuesday	Ac 4:32-37	IV, 52		Jn 3:7-15	IV, 54
Wednesday	Ac 5:17-26	IV, 54		Jn 3:16-21	IV, 55
Thursday	Ac 5:27-33	IV, 55		Jn 3:31-36	IV, 56
Friday	Ac 5:34-42	IV, 56		Jn 6:1-15	IV, 57
Saturday	Ac 6:1-7	IV, 59		Jn 6:16-21	IV, 60

	1st reading		*Gospel*	
Third Week of Easter				
Monday	Ac 6:8-15	IV, 97	Jn 6:22-29	IV, 98
Tuesday	Ac 7:51-59	IV, 99	Jn 6:30-35	IV, 99
Wednesday	Ac 8:1-8	IV, 101	Jn 6:35-40	IV, 101
Thursday	Ac 8:26-40	IV, 102	Jn 6:44-51	IV, 104
Friday	Ac 9:1-20	IV, 106	Jn 6:53-60	IV, 109
Saturday	Ac 9:31-42	IV, 110	Jn 6:61-70	IV, 112
Fourth Week of Easter				
Monday	Ac 11:1-18	IV, 139	Jn 10:1-10 or 10:11-18	IV, 141
Tuesday	Ac 11:19-26	IV, 141	Jn 10:22-30	IV, 144
Wednesday	Ac 12:24-13:5	IV, 144	Jn 12:44-50	IV, 145
Thursday	Ac 13:13-25	IV, 146	Jn 13:16-20	IV, 148
Friday	Ac 13:16, 26-33	IV, 149	Jn 14:1-6	IV, 152
Saturday	Ac 13:44-52	IV, 152	Jn 14:7-14	IV, 152
Fifth Week of Easter				
Monday	Ac 14:5-17	IV, 184	Jn 14:21-26	IV, 186
Tuesday	Ac 14:18-27	IV, 186	Jn 14:27-31	IV, 186
Wednesday	Ac 15:1-6	IV, 187	Jn 15:1-8	IV, 188
Thursday	Ac 15:7-21	IV, 188	Jn 15:9-11	IV, 191
Friday	Ac 15:22-31	IV, 191	Jn 15:12-17	IV, 191
Saturday	Ac 16:1-10	IV, 192	Jn 15:18-21	IV, 194
Sixth Week of Easter				
Monday	Ac 16:11-15	IV, 220	Jn 15:26-16:4	IV, 221
Tuesday	Ac 16:22-34	IV, 222	Jn 16:5-11	IV, 223
Wednesday	Ac 17:15, 22-18:1	IV, 225	Jn 16:12-15	IV, 227
Thursday			Jn 16:16-20	IV, 244
Friday	Ac 18:9-18	IV, 240	Jn 16:20-23	IV, 240
Saturday	Ac 18:23-28	IV, 242	Jn 16:23-28	IV, 243
Seventh Week of Easter				
Monday	Ac 19:1-8	IV, 279	Jn 16:29-33	IV, 280
Tuesday	Ac 20:17-27	IV, 281	Jn 17:1-11	IV, 283
Wednesday	Ac 20:28-38	IV, 284	Jn 17:11-19	IV, 285
Thursday	Ac 22:30; 23:6-11	IV, 286	Jn 17:20-26	IV, 286
Friday	Ac 25:13-21	IV, 287	Jn 21:15-19	IV, 287
Saturday	Ac 28:16-20; 30-31	IV, 287	Jn 21:20-25	IV, 289

* * *

First Week

	1st reading (I)		*1st reading (II)*		*Gospel*	
Mon	Heb 1:1-6	II, 1	1 S 1:1-8	II, 3	Mk 1:14-20	II, 3
Tues	Heb 2:5-12	II, 4	1 S 1:9-20	II, 5	Mk 1:21-28	II, 6
Wed	Heb 2:14-18	II, 6	1 S 3:1-10, 19-20	II, 7	Mk 1:29-39	II, 7
Thurs	Heb 3:7-14	II, 8	1 S 4:1c-11	II, 10	Mk 1:40-45	II, 11
Fri	Heb 4:1-5, 11	II, 12	1 S 8:4-7, 10-22a	II, 13	Mk 2:1-12	II, 15
Sat	Heb 4:12-16	II, 15	1 S 9:1-4, 17-19; 10:1	II, 17	Mk 2:13-17	II, 18

Second Week

Mon	Heb 5:1-10	II, 48	1 S 15:16-23	II, 49	Mk 2:18-22	II, 51
Tues	Heb 6:10-20	II, 51	1 S 16:1-13	II, 52	Mk 2:23-28	II, 53
Wed	Heb 7:1-3, 15-17	II, 55	1 S 17:32-33, 37, 40-51	II, 56	Mk 3:1-6	II, 57
Thurs	Heb 7:25-8:6	II, 59	1 S 18:6-9; 19:1-7	II, 60	Mk 3:7-12	II, 60
Fri	Heb 8:6-13	II, 62	1 S 24:3-21	II, 63	Mk 3:13-19	II, 64
Sat	Heb 9:2-3, 11-14	II, 67	2 S 1:1-4, 11-12 19:23-27	II, 70	Mk 3:20-21	II, 71

Third Week

Mon	Heb 9:15; 24-28	II, 100	2 S 5:1-7, 10	II, 101	Mk 3:22-30	II, 102
Tues	Heb 10:1-10	II, 104	2 S 6:12b-15, 17-19	II, 106	Mk 3:31-35	II, 107
Wed	Heb 10:11-18	II, 107	2 S 7:4-17	II, 109	Mk 4:1-20	II, 110
Thurs	Heb 10:19-25	II, 113	2 S 7:18-19, 24-29	II, 115	Mk 4:21-25	II, 116
Fri	Heb 10:32-39	II, 117	2 S 11:1-4a, 5-10a, 13-17	II, 118	Mk 4:26-34	II, 119
Sat	Heb 11:1-2, 8-19	II, 121	2 S 12:1-7a, 10-17	II, 123	Mk 4:35-41	II, 125

Fourth Week

Mon	Heb 11:32-40	II, 154	2 S 15:13-14, 30; 16:5-13a	II, 155	Mk 5:1-20	II, 156

	1st reading (I)		*1st reading (II)*		*Gospel*	
Tues	Heb 12:1-4	II, 158	2 S 18:9-10, 14b, 24-25a, 30-19:3	II, 159	Mk 5:21-43	II, 160
Wed	Heb 12:4-7, 11-15	II, 161	2 S 24:2, 9-17	II, 162	Mk 6:1-6	II, 163
Thurs	Heb 12:18-19, 21-24	II, 165	1 K 2:1-4, 10-12	II, 166	Mk 6:7-13	II, 167
Fri	Heb 13:1-8	II, 170	Si 47:2-13	II, 171	Mk 6:14-29	II, 173
Sat	Heb 13:15-17, 20-21	II, 174	1 K 3:4-13	II, 175	Mk 6:30-34	II, 176

Fifth Week

Mon	Gn 1:1-19	II, 202	1 K 8:1-7, 9-13	II, 204	Mk 6:53-56	II, 205
Tues	Gn 1:20-2:4a	II, 207	1 K 8:22-23, 27-30	II, 210	Mk 7:1-13	II, 211
Wed	Gn 2:4b-9, 15-17	II, 213	1 K 10:1-10	II, 215	Mk 7:14-23	II, 216
Thurs	Gn 2:18-25	II, 218	1 K 11:4-13	II, 219	Mk 7:24-30	II, 221
Fri	Gn 3:1-8	II, 223	1 K 11:29-32, 12:19	II, 225	Mk 7:31-37	II, 226
Sat	Gn 3:9-24	II, 229	1 K 12:26-32; 13:33-34	II, 232	Mk 8:1-10	II, 233

Sixth Week

Mon	Gn 4:1-15, 25	II, 261	Jm 1:1-11	II, 262	Mk 8:11-13	II, 263
Tues	Gn 6:5-8, 7:1-5, 10	II, 265	Jm 1:12-18	II, 265	Mk 8:14-21	II, 267
Wed	Gn 8:6-13, 20-22	II, 267	Jm 1:19-27	II, 269	Mk 8:22-26	II, 271
Thurs	Gn 9:1-13	II, 273	Jm 2:1-9	II, 275	Mk 8:27-33	II, 276
Fri	Gn 11:1-9	II, 278	Jm 2:14-24, 26	II, 280	Mk 8:34-38	II, 281
Sat	Heb 11:1-7	II, 283	Jm 3:1-10	II, 285	Mk 9:1-12	II, 286

Seventh Week

Mon	Si 1:1-10	II, 306	Jm 3:13-18	II, 307	Mk 9:14-29	II, 308
Tues	Si 2:1-11	II, 310	Jm 4:1-10	II, 311	Mk 9:30-37	II, 312
Wed	Si 4:11-19	II, 314	Jm 4:13-17	II, 314	Mk 9:38-40	II, 316
Thurs	Si 5:1-8	II, 316	Jm 5:1-6	II, 318	Mk 9:41-50	II, 319
Fri	Si 6:5-17	II, 320	Jm 5:9-12	II, 321	Mk 10:1-12	II, 321
Sat	Si 17:1-15	II, 323	Jm 5:13-20	II, 324	Mk 10:13-16	II, 327

Eighth Week

	1st reading (I)		*1st reading (II)*		*Gospel*	
Mon	Si 17:19-27	II, 347	1 P 1:3-9	II, 347	Mk 10:17-27	II, 349
Tues	Si 35:1-12	II, 353	1 P 1:10-16	II, 354	Mk 10:28-31	II, 356
Wed	Si 36:1, 5-6, 10-17	II, 359	1 P 1:18-25	II, 360	Mk 10:32-45	II, 362
Thurs	Si 42:15-25	II, 366	1 P 2:2-5, 9-12	II, 366	Mk 10:46-52	II, 369
Fri	Si 44:1, 9-13	II, 370	1 P 4:7-13	II, 371	Mk 11:11-26	II, 372
Sat	Si 51:12-20	II, 375	Jude 17:20-25	II, 376	Mk 11:27-33	II, 377

Ninth Week

	1st reading (I)		*1st reading (II)*		*Gospel*	
Mon	Tb 1:1-2; 2:1-9	VI, 1	2 P 1:2-7	VI, 2	Mk 12:1-12	VI, 3
Tues	Tb 2:9-14	VI, 4	2 P 3:12-15, 17-18	VI, 5	Mk 12:13-17	VI, 5
Wed	Tb 3:1-11, 16	VI, 7	2 Tm 1:1-3, 6-12	VI, 9	Mk 12:18-27	VI, 12
Thurs	Tb 6:10-11; 7:1, 9-17; 8:4-10	VI, 14	2 Tm 2:8-15	VI, 17	Mk 12:28-34	VI, 18
Fri	Tb 11:5-17	VI, 19	2 Tm 3:10-17	VI, 20	Mk 12:35-37	VI, 23
Sat	Tb 12:1, 5-15, 20	VI, 24	2 Tm 4:1-8	VI, 24	Mk 12:38-44	VI, 25

Tenth Week

	1st reading (I)		*1st reading (II)*		*Gospel*	
Mon	2 Co 1:1-7	VI, 27	1 K 17:1-6	VI, 28	Mt 5:1-12a	VI, 29
Tues	2 Co 1:18-22	VI, 31	1 K 17:7-16	VI, 33	Mt 5:13-16	VI, 34
Wed	2 Co 3:4-11	VI, 35	1 K 18:20-39	VI, 37	Mt 5:17-20	VI, 38
Thurs	2 Co 3:15-4:6	VI, 40	1 K 18:41-46	VI, 42	Mt 5:20-26	VI, 42
Fri	2 Co 4:7-15	VI, 45	1 K 19:9-16	VI, 47	Mt 5:27-32	VI, 48
Sat	2 Co 5:14-21	VI, 50	1 K 19:16, 19-21	VI, 52	Mt 5:33-37	VI, 53

Eleventh Week

	1st reading (I)		*1st reading (II)*		*Gospel*	
Mon	2 Co 6:1-10	VI, 54	1 K 21:1-16	VI, 55	Mt 5:38-42a, 43-48	VI, 57
Tues	2 Co 8:1-9	VI, 59	1 K 21:17-29	VI, 61	Mt 5:43-48	VI, 61
Wed	2 Co 9:6-11	VI, 61	2 K 2:1, 6-14	VI, 62	Mt 6:1-6, 16-18	VI, 63
Thurs	2 Co 11:1-11	VI, 65	Si 48:1-15	VI, 66	Mt 6:7-15	VI, 67
Fri	2 Co 11:18-30	VI, 70	2 K 11:1-4, 9-18, 20	VI, 72	Mt 6:19-23	VI, 73
Sat	2 Co 12:1-10	VI, 74	2 Ch 24:17-25	VI, 76	Mt 6:24-34	VI, 76

Twelfth Week

	1st reading (I)		*1st reading (II)*		*Gospel*	
Mon	Gn 12:1-9	VI, 81	2 K 17:5-8, 13-15, 18	VI, 83	Mt 7:1-5	VI, 84
Tues	Gn 13:2, 5-18	VI, 84	2 K 19:9-11, 14-21, 31-36	VI, 85	Mt 7:6, 12-14	VI, 86
Wed	Gn 15:1-12, 17-18	VI, 86	2 K 22:8-13; 23:1-3	VI, 89	Mt 7:15-20	VI, 90
Thurs	Gn 16:1-12	VI, 91	2 K 24:8-17	VI, 92	Mt 7:21-29	VI, 93
Fri	Gn 17:1, 9-12, 15-22	VI, 94	2 K 25:1-12	VI, 97	Mt 8:1-4	VI, 98
Sat	Gn 18:1-15	VI, 100	Lm 2:2, 10-14, 18-19	VI, 102	Mt 8:5-17	VI, 102

Thirteenth Week

Mon	Gn 18:16-33	VI, 105	Am 2:6-10, 13-16	VI, 107	Mt 8:18-22	VI, 107
Tues	Gn 19:15-29	VI, 108	Am 3:1-8, 4:11-12	VI, 110	Mt 8:23-27	VI, 110
Wed	Gn 21:8-20	VI, 112	Am 5:14-15, 21-24	VI, 112	Mt 8:28-34	VI, 113
Thurs	Gn 22:1-19	VI, 115	Am 7:10-19	VI, 117	Mt 9:1-8	VI, 118
Fri	Gn 23:1-4, 19; 24:1-8, 62-67	VI, 120	Am 8:4-6, 9:12	VI, 121	Mt 9:9-13	VI, 122
Sat	Gn 27:1-5, 15-29	VI, 123	Am 9:11-15	VI, 124	Mt 9:14-17	VI, 126

Fourteenth Week

Mon	Gn 28:10-22	VI, 129	Ho 2:18-25	VI, 130	Mt 9:18-26	VI, 132
Tues	Gn 32:23-33	VI, 133	Ho 8:4-7, 11-13	VI, 134	Mt 9:32-38	VI, 139
Wed	Gn 41:55-57; 42:5-7, 17-24	VI, 141	Ho 10:1-3, 7-8, 12	VI, 142	Mt 10:1-7	VI, 143
Thurs	Gn 44:18-29; 45:1-5	VI, 144	Ho 11:1-9	VI, 144	Mt 10:7-15	VI, 145
Fri	Gn 46:1-7, 28-30	VI, 147	Ho 14:2-10	VI, 148	Mt 10:16-23	VI, 150
Sat	Gn 49:29-33; 50:15-24	VI, 152	Is 6:1-8	VI, 153	Mt 10:24-33	VI, 155

Fifteenth Week

Mon	Ex 1:8-14, 22	VI, 158	Is 1:11-17	VI, 159	Mt 10:34-11:1	VI, 160

	1st reading (I)		*1st reading (II)*		*Gospel*	
Tues	Ex 2:1-15	VI, 161	Is 7:1-9	VI, 162	Mt 11:20-24	VI, 163
Wed	Ex 3:1-6, 9-12	VI, 164	Is 10:5-7, 13-16	VI, 167	Mt 11:25-30	VI, 168
Thurs	Ex 3:13-20	VI, 170	Is 26:7-9, 12-16, 19	VI, 172	Mt 11:28-30	VI, 173
Fri	Ex 11:10-12, 14	VI, 173	Is 38:1-6, 21-22, 7-8	VI, 175	Mt 12:1-8	VI, 176
Sat	Ex 12:37-42	VI, 178	Mi 2:1-5	VI, 179	Mt 12:14-21	VI, 179

Sixteenth Week

Mon	Ex 14:5-18	VI, 188	Mi 6:1-8	VI, 190	Mt 12:38-42	VI, 190
Tues	Ex 14:21-15:1	VI, 193	Mi 7:14-15, 18-20	VI, 194	Mt 12:46-50	VI, 195
Wed	Ex 16:1-5, 9-15	VI, 196	Jr 1:1, 4-10	VI, 198	Mt 13:1-9	VI, 199
Thurs	Ex 19:1-11, 16-20	VI, 200	Jr 2:1-3, 7-8, 12-13	VI, 202	Mt 13:10-17	VI, 203
Fri	Ex 20:1-17	VI, 206	Jr 3:14-17	VI, 209	Mt 13:18-23	VI, 210
Sat	Ex 24:3-8	VI, 210	Jr 7:1-11	VI, 212	Mt 13:24-30	VI, 212

Seventeenth Week

Mon	Ex 32:15-24, 30-34	VI, 215	Jr 13:1-11	VI, 216	Mt 13:31-35	VI, 216
Tues	Ex 33:7-11; 34:5-9, 28	VI, 218	Jr 14:17-22	VI, 219	Mt 13:36-43	VI, 220
Wed	Ex 34:29-35	VI, 220	Jr 15:10, 16-21	VI, 220	Mt 13:44-46	VI, 221
Thurs	Ex 40:16-21, 34-38	VI, 222	Jr 18:1-6	VI, 224	Mt 13:47-53	VI, 225
Fri	Lv 23:1, 4-11, 15-16, 27, 34-37	VI, 225	Jr 26:1-9	VI, 227	Mt 13:54-58	VI, 228
Sat	Lv 25:1, 8-17	VI, 229	Jr 26:11-16, 24	VI, 231	Mt 14:1-12	VI, 232

Eighteenth Week

Mon	Nb 11:4-15	VI, 236	Jr 28:1-17	VI, 237	Mt 14:13-21	VI, 238
Tues	Nb 12:1-13	VI, 240	Jr 30:1-2, 12-15, 18-22	VI, 240	Mt 14:22-36	VI, 242
Wed	Nb 13:1-2, 25-14:1, 26-29, 34-35	VI, 243	Jr 31:1-7	VI, 245	Mt 15:21-28	VI, 245
Thurs	Nb 20:1-13	VI, 246	Jr 31:31-34	VI, 248	Mt 16:13-23	VI, 249

	1st reading (I)		*1st reading (II)*		*Gospel*	
Fri	Dt 4:32-34, 38-40	VI, 251	Na 2:1,3; 3:1-3, 6-7	VI, 252	Mt 16:24-28	VI, 253
Sat	Dt 6:4-13	VI, 255	Ha 1:12-2:4	VI, 257	Mt 17:14-20	VI, 258
Nineteenth Week						
Mon	Dt 10:12-22	VI, 261	Ez 1:2-5, 24-28	VI, 262	Mt 17:22-27	VI, 262
Tues	Dt 31:1-8	VI, 264	Ez 2:8, 3:4	VI, 265	Mt 18:1-5, 10, 12-14	VI, 266
Wed	Dt 34:1-12	VI, 269	Ez 9:1-7, 10:18-22	VI, 270	Mt 18:15-20	VI, 271
Thurs	Jos 3:7-17	VI, 273	Ez 12:1-12	VI, 274	Mt 18:21-19:1	VI, 275
Fri	Jos 24:1-15	VI, 277	Ez 16:1-15, 60-63	VI, 279	Mt 19:3-12	VI, 281
Sat	Jos 24:14-29	VI, 283	Ez 18:1-10, 26-32	VI, 283	Mt 19:13-15	VI, 284
Twentieth Week						
Mon	Jg 2:11-19	VI, 286	Ez 24:15-24	VI, 287	Mt 19:16-22	VI, 288
Tues	Jg 6:11-24	VI, 289	Ez 28:1-10	VI, 290	Mt 19:23-30	VI, 290
Wed	Jg 9:6-15	VI, 292	Ez 34:1-11	VI, 293	Mt 20:1-16	VI, 294
Thurs	Jg 11:29-38	VI, 296	Ez 36:23-28	VI, 296	Mt 22:1-14	VI, 297
Fri	Rt 1:1-6, 14-16, 22	VI, 301	Ez 37:1-14	VI, 302	Mt 22:34-40	VI, 303
Sat	Rt 2:1-3, 8-11, 4:13-17	VI, 304	Ez 43:1-7	VI, 304	Mt 23:1-12	VI, 305
Twenty-First Week						
Mon	1 Th 1:2-5; 8-10	VI, 307	2 Th 1:1-5, 11-19	VI, 308	Mt 23:13-22	VI, 309
Tues	1 Th 2:1-8	VI, 311	2 Th 2:1-3, 13-16	VI, 313	Mt 23:23-26	VI, 316
Wed	1 Th 2:9-13	VI, 317	2 Th 3:6-10, 16-18	VI, 319	Mt 23:27-32	VI, 322
Thurs	1 Th 3:7-13	VI, 322	1 Co 1:1-9	VI, 324	Mt 24:42-51	VI, 326
Fri	1 Th 4:1-8	VI, 328	1 Co 1:17-25	VI, 330	Mt 25:1-13	VI, 332
Sat	1 Th 4:9-12	VI, 333	1 Co 1:26-31	VI, 334	Mt 25:14-30	VI, 336
Twenty-Second Week						
Mon	1 Th 4:13-18	VIII, 1	1 Co 2:1-5	VIII, 2	Lk 4:16-30	VIII, 3
Tues	1 Th 5:1-6, 9-11	VIII, 6	1 Co 2:10-16	VIII, 7	Lk 4:31-37	VIII, 8

	1st reading (I)		*1st reading (II)*		*Gospel*	
Wed	Col 1:1-8	VIII, 9	1 Co 3:1-9	VIII, 10	Lk 4:38-44	VIII, 11
Thurs	Col 1:9-14	VIII, 12	1 Co 3:18-23	VIII, 13	Lk 5:1-11	VIII, 14
Fri	Col 1:15-20	VIII, 16	1 Co 4:1-5	VIII, 18	Lk 5:33-39	VIII, 18
Sat	Col 1:21-23	VIII, 20	1 Co 4:6-15	VIII, 21	Lk 6:1-5	VIII, 23

Twenty-Third Week

Mon	Col 1:24-2:3	VIII, 25	1 Co 5:1-8	VIII, 26	Lk 6:6-11	VIII, 28
Tues	Col 2:6-15	VIII, 30	1 Co 6:1-11	VIII, 32	Lk 6:12-19	VIII, 34
Wed	Col 3:1-11	VIII, 36	1 Co 7:25-31	VIII, 38	Lk 6:20-26	VIII, 40
Thurs	Col 3:12-17	VIII, 42	1 Co 8:1b-7, 11-13	VIII, 44	Lk 6:27-38	VIII, 45
Fri	1 Tm 1:1-2, 12-14	VIII, 46	1 Co 9:16-19, 22-27	VIII, 47	Lk 6:39-42	VIII, 49
Sat	1 Tm 1:15-17	VIII, 49	1 Co 10:10-22a	VIII, 51	Lk 6:43-49	VIII, 52

Twenty-Fourth Week

Mon	1 Tm 2:1-8	VIII, 54	1 Co 11:17-26, 33	VIII, 55	Lk 7:1-10	VIII, 57
Tues	1 Tm 3:1-13	VIII, 59	1 Co 12:12-14, 27-31a	VIII, 60	Lk 7:11-17	VIII, 61
Wed	1 Tm 3:14-16	VIII, 63	1 Co 12:31-13:13	VIII, 65	Lk 7:31-35	VIII, 67
Thurs	1 Tm 4:12-16	VIII, 68	1 Co 15:1-11	VIII, 69	Lk 7:36-50	VIII, 71
Fri	1 Tm 6:2c-12	VIII, 74	1 Co 15:12-20	VIII, 75	Lk 8:1-3	VIII, 76
Sat	1 Tm 6:13-16	VIII, 77	1 Co 15:35-37, 42-49	VIII, 78	Lk 8:4-15	VIII, 80

Twenty-Fifth Week

Mon	Ezr 1:1-6	VIII, 83	Pr 3:27-34	VIII, 84	Lk 8:16-18	VIII, 84
Tues	Ezr 6:7-8, 12b, 14-20	VIII, 86	Pr 21:1-6, 10-13	VIII, 87	Lk 8:19-21	VIII, 87
Wed	Ezr 9:5-9	VIII, 88	Pr 30:5-9	VIII, 89	Lk 9:1-6	VIII, 89
Thurs	Hg 1:1-8	VIII, 91	Ec 1:2-11	VIII, 92	Lk 9:7-9	VIII, 93

	1st reading (I)		1st reading (II)		Gospel	
Fri	Hg 2:1b-10	VIII, 95	Ec 3:1-11	VIII, 96	Lk 9:18-22	VIII, 97
Sat	Zc 2:5-9, 10-11a	VIII, 100	Ec 11:9-12:8	VIII, 101	Lk 9:44b-45	VIII, 101
Twenty-Sixth Week						
Mon	Zc 8:1-8	VIII, 103	Jb 1:6-22	VIII, 103	Lk 9:46-50	VIII, 104
Tues	Zc 8:20-23	VIII, 105	Jb 3:1-2, 11-17, 20-23	VIII, 106	Lk 9:51-56	VIII, 107
Wed	Ne 2:1-8	VIII, 108	Jb 9:1-12, 14-16	VIII, 108	Lk 9:57-62	VIII, 110
Thurs	Ne 8:1-4a, 5-6, 7b-12	VIII, 111	Jb 19:21-27	VIII, 112	Lk 10:1-12	VIII, 113
Fri	Ba 1:15-22	VIII, 116	Jb 38:1, 12-21; 39:33-35	VIII, 117	Lk 10:13-16	VIII, 117
Sat	Ba 4:5-12, 27-29	VIII, 119	Jb 42:1-3, 5-6, 12-17	VIII, 120	Lk 10:17-24	VIII, 121
Twenty-Seventh Week						
Mon	Jon 1:1-2:1, 11	VIII, 122	Ga 1:6-12	VIII, 122	Lk 10:25-37	VIII, 124
Tues	Jon 3:1-10	VIII, 127	Ga 1:13-24	VIII, 128	Lk 10:38-42	VIII, 130
Wed	Jon 4:1-11	VIII, 131	Ga 2:1-2, 7-14	VIII, 132	Lk 11:1-4	VIII, 134
Thurs	Ml 3:13-20a	VIII, 136	Ga 3:1-5	VIII, 137	Lk 11:5-13	VIII, 137
Fri	Jl 1:13-15, 2:1-2	VIII, 139	Ga 3:7-14	VIII, 140	Lk 11:15-26	VIII, 142
Sat	Jl 4:12-21	VIII, 144	Ga 3:22-29	VIII, 146	Lk 11:27-28	VIII, 148
Twenty-Eighth Week						
Mon	Rm 1:1-7	VIII, 149	Ga 4:22-24, 26-27, 31-5:1	VIII, 151	Lk 11:29-32	VIII, 152
Tues	Rm 1:16-25	VIII, 155	Ga 5:1-6	VIII, 157	Lk 11:37-41	VIII, 159
Wed	Rm 2:1-11	VIII, 160	Ga 5:18-25	VIII, 161	Lk 11:42-46	VIII, 162
Thurs	Rm 3:21-30a	VIII, 164	Ep 1:1-10	VIII, 166	Lk 11:47-54	VIII, 169

	1st reading (I)		*1st reading (II)*		*Gospel*	
Fri	Rm 4:1-8	VIII, 170	Ep 1:11-14	VIII, 171	Lk 12:1-7	VIII, 172
Sat	Rm 4:13, 16-18	VIII, 173	Ep 1:15-23	VIII, 175	Lk 12:8-12	VIII, 176

Twenty-Ninth Week

Mon	Rm 4:20-25	VIII, 178	Ep 2:1-10	VIII, 179	Lk 12:13-21	VIII, 180
Tues	Rm 5:12-15b, 17-19, 20b-21	VIII, 182	Ep 2:12-22	VIII, 185	Lk 12:35-38	VIII, 187
Wed	Rm 6:12-18	VIII, 188	Ep 3:2-12	VIII, 189	Lk 12:39-48	VIII, 190
Thurs	Rm 6:19-23	VIII, 191	Ep 3:14-21	VIII, 192	Lk 12:49-53	VIII, 193
Fri	Rm 7:18-25a	VIII, 194	Ep 4:1-6	VIII, 197	Lk 12:54-59	VIII, 198
Sat	Rm 8:1-11	VIII, 199	Ep 4:7-16	VIII, 201	Lk 13:1-9	VIII, 203

Thirtieth Week

Mon	Rm 8:12-17	VIII, 205	Ep 4:32-5:8	VIII, 207	Lk 13:10-17	VIII, 208
Tues	Rm 8:18-25	VIII, 208	Ep 5:21-33	VIII, 210	Lk 13:18-21	VIII, 212
Wed	Rm 8:26-30	VIII, 214	Ep 6:1-9	VIII, 216	Lk 13:22-30	VIII, 218
Thurs	Rm 8:31b-39	VIII, 220	Ep 6:10-20	VIII, 222	Lk 13:31-35	VIII, 223
Fri	Rm 9:1-5	VIII, 224	Ph 1:1-11	VIII, 226	Lk 14:1-6	VIII, 227
Sat	Rm 11:1-2a, 11-12, 25-29	VIII, 228	Ph 1:18b-26	VIII, 230	Lk 14:1, 7-11	VIII, 231

Thirty-First Week

Mon	Rm 11:29-36	VIII, 232	Ph 2:1-4	VIII, 233	Lk 14:12-14, 15-24	VIII, 234
Tues	Rm 12:5-16a	VIII, 237	Ph 2:5-11	VIII, 239	Lk 14:15-24	VIII, 240
Wed	Rm 13:8-10	VIII, 241	Ph 2:12-18	VIII, 242	Lk 14:25-33	VIII, 242
Thurs	Rm 14:7-12	VIII, 244	Ph 3:3-8a	VIII, 245	Lk 15:1-10	VIII, 246

	1st reading (I)		*1st reading (II)*		*Gospel*	
Fri	Rm 15:14-21	VIII, 248	Ph 3:17-4:1	VIII, 249	Lk 16:1-8	VIII, 250
Sat	Rm 16:3-9, 16, 22-27	VIII, 252	Ph 4:10-19	VIII, 253	Lk 16:9-15	VIII, 254
Thirty-Second Week						
Mon	Ws 1:1-7	VIII, 256	Tt 1:1-9	VIII, 257	Lk 17:1-6	VIII, 258
Tues	Ws 2:23-3:9	VIII, 259	Tt 2:1-8, 11-14	VIII, 260	Lk 17:7-10	VIII, 261
Wed	Ws 6:1-11	VIII, 262	Tt 3:1-7	VIII, 263	Lk 17:11-19	VIII, 264
Thurs	Ws 7:22-8:1	VIII, 265	Phm 7-20	VIII, 267	Lk 17:20-25	VIII, 268
Fri	Ws 13:1-9	VIII, 270	2 Jn 4-9	VIII, 271	Lk 17:26-37	VIII, 272
Sat	Ws 18:14-16; 19:6-9	VIII, 273	3 Jn 5-8	VIII, 275	Lk 18:1-8	VIII, 276
Thirty-Third Week						
Mon	1 M 1:10-15, 41-43, 54-57, 62-64	VIII, 278	Rv 1:1-4; 2:1-5a	VIII, 280	Lk 18:35-43	VIII, 281
Tues	2 M 6:18-31	VIII, 283	Rv 3:1-6, 14-22	VIII, 284	Lk 19:1-10	VIII, 285
Wed	2 M 7:1, 20-31	VIII, 287	Rv 4:1-11	VIII, 288	Lk 19:11-28	VIII, 290
Thurs	1 M 2:15-29	VIII, 291	Rv 5:1-10	VIII, 292	Lk 19:41-44	VIII, 293
Fri	1 M 4:36-37, 52-59	VIII, 296	Rv 10:8-11	VIII, 297	Lk 19:45-48	VIII, 298
Sat	1 M 6:1-13	VIII, 300	Rv 11:4-12	VIII, 300	Lk 20:27-40	VIII, 301
Thirty-Fourth (and Last) Week						
Mon	Dn 1:1-6, 8-20	VIII, 303	Rv 14:1-3, 4b-5	VIII, 305	Lk 21:1-4	VIII, 305
Tues	Dn 2:31-45	VIII, 306	Rv 14:14-19	VIII, 308	Lk 21:5-11	VIII, 308
Wed	Dn 5:1-6, 13-14, 16-17, 23-28	VIII, 310	Rv 15:1-4	VIII, 311	Lk 21:12-19	VIII, 311

	1st reading (I)		*1st reading (II)*		*Gospel*	
Thurs	Dn 6:12-28	VIII, 311	Rv 18:1-2, 21-23; 19:1-3, 9a	VIII, 312	Lk 21:20-28	VIII, 313
Fri	Dn 7:2-14	VIII, 314	Rv 20:1-4, 11-21:2	VIII, 315	Lk 21:29-33	VIII, 318
Sat	Dn 7:15-27	VIII, 320	Rv 22:1-7	VIII, 320	Lk 21:34-36	VIII, 320

III. THE LECTIONARY OF COMMONS

A. DEDICATION OF A CHURCH

First Reading

a) Outside of Eastertime:

	Reading	Ref.
1.	Gn 28:11-18	VI, 129
2.	1 K 8:22-23, 27-30	II, 210
3.	2 Ch 5:6-10, 13-6:2	—
4.	1 M 4:52-59	VIII, 296
5.	Is 56:1, 6-7	V, 296
6.	Ez 43:1-2, 4-7a	VI, 304

b) In Eastertime:

	Reading	Ref.
1.	Ac 7:44-50	—
2.	Rv 8:3-4	—
3.	Rv 21:1-5a	IV, 162
4.	Rv 21:9b-14	IV, 200

Second Reading

	Reading	Ref.
1.	1 Co 3:9b-13, 16-17	II, 292
2.	Ep 2:19-22	VIII, 185
3.	Heb 12:18-19, 22-24	VII, 8
4.	1 P 2:4-9	IV, 159

Gospel

	Reading	Ref.
1.	Mt 5:23-24	III, 54
2.	Lk 19:1-10	VII, 235
3.	Jn 2:13-22	III, 127
4.	Jn 4:19-24	III, 123

B. COMMON OF THE BLESSED VIRGIN MARY

First Reading

a) Outside of Eastertime:

	Reading	Ref.
1.	Gn 3:9-15, 20	V, 32
2.	Gn 12:1-7	VI, 81
3.	2 S 7:1-5, 8b-11, 16	I, 131, 173
4.	1 Ch 15:3-4, 15-16; 16:1-2	—
5.	Pr 8:22-31	IV, 316
6.	Si 24:1-4, 8-12, 19-22	I, 278
7.	Is 7:10-14	I, 130
8.	Is 9:2-7	I, 178
9.	Is 61:9-11	I, 91
10.	Mi 5:2-5a	I, 134
11.	Zc 2:10-13	VIII, 100

b) In Eastertime:

	Reading	Ref.
1.	Ac 1:12-14	IV, 251
2.	Rv 11:19a; 12:1-6a, 10ab	—
3.	Rv 21:1-5a	IV, 162

Second Reading

	Reading	Ref.
1.	Rm 5:12, 17-19	III, 12
2.	Rm 8:28-30	V, 220
3.	Ga 4:4-7	I, 241
4.	Ep 1:3-6, 11-12	V, 170

Gospel

	Reading	Ref.
1.	Mt 1:1-16, 18-23	I, 160
2.	Mt 2:13-15, 19-23	I, 202
3.	Lk 1:26-38	I, 142
4.	Lk 1:39-47	I, 146
5.	Lk 2:1-14	I, 187
6.	Lk 2:15b-19	I, 244
7.	Lk 2:27-35	I, 233
8.	Lk 2:41-52	I, 209
9.	Lk 11:27-28	VIII, 148
10.	Jn 2:1-11	II, 34
11.	Jn 19:25-27	—

C. COMMON OF MARTYRS

First Reading

a) Outside of Eastertime:

	Reading	Ref.
1.	2 Ch 24:18-22	VI, 76
2.	2 M 6:18, 21, 24-31	VIII, 283
3.	2 M 7:1-2, 9-14	VII, 250
4.	2 M 7:1, 20-23, 27b-29	—
5.	Ws 3:1-9c	VIII, 259
6.	Ws 51:1-8	—

b) In Eastertime:

1. Ac 7:55-8:1a	—
2. Rv 7:9-17	IV, 119
3. Rv 12:10-12a	—
4. Rv 21:5-7	—

Second Reading

1. Rm 5:1-5	III, 117
2. Rm 8:31b-39	VIII, 220
3. 2 Co 4:7-15	VI, 45
4. 2 Co 6:4-10	VI, 54
5. 2 Tm 2:8-13; 3:10-12	VII, 159
6. Heb 10:32-36	II, 117
7. Jm 1:2-4, 12	II, 262
8. 1 P 3:14-17	IV, 198
9. 1 P 4:12-19	IV, 256
10. 1 Jn 5:1-5	IV, 28

Gospel

1. Mt 10:17-22	I, 224
2. Mt 10:28-33	V, 95
3. Mt 10:34-39	VI, 160
4. Lk 9:23-26	III, 3
5. Jn 12:24-26	III, 217
6. Jn 15:18-21	IV, 194
7. Jn 17:11b-19	IV, 261

D. COMMON OF PASTORS

(M)—For Missionaries
(P)—For Popes

First Reading

a) Outside of Eastertime:

1. Ex 32:7-14	III, 199
2. Dt 10:8-9	—
3. 1 S 16:1b, 6-13a	II, 52
4. Is 6:1-8	VI, 153
5. Is 52:7-10 (M)	I, 181
6. Is 61:1-3a	I, 91
7. Jr 1:4-9	VI, 198
8. Ez 3:16-21	—
9. Ez 34:11-16	IV, 360

b) In Eastertime:

1. Ac 13:46-49 (M)	IV, 152
2. Ac 20:17-18a, 28-32, 36	IV, 281
3. Ac 26:19-23 (M)	—

Second Reading

1. Rm 12:3-13	VIII, 237
2. 1 Co 1:18-25 (M)	VI, 330
3. 1 Co 4:1-5	II, 331
4. 1 Co 9:16-19, 22-23	VIII, 47
5. 2 Co 3:1-6a	II, 332
6. 2 Co 4:1-2, 5-7	VI, 40
7. 2 Co 5:14-20	VI, 50
8. Ep 4:1-7, 11-13	VIII, 197 and 201
9. Col 1:24-29	V, 199
10. 1 Th 2:2b-8	VI, 311
11. 2 Tm 1:13-14; 2:1-3	—
12. 2 Tm 4:1-5	VI, 24
13. 1 P 5:1-4	—

Gospel

1. Mt 16:13-19 (P)	V, 329
2. Mt 23:8-12	III, 95
3. Mt 28:16-20 (M)	IV, 232
4. Mk 1:14-20	II, 3
5. Mk 16:15-20 (M)	IV, 234
6. Lk 5:1-11 (M)	II, 188
7. Lk 10:1-9	V, 151
8. Lk 22:24-30	—
9. Jn 10:11-16	IV, 123 and 141
10. Jn 15:9-17	IV, 203
11. Jn 21:15-17 (P)	IV, 287

E. COMMON OF DOCTORS

First Reading

a) Outside of Eastertime:

1. 1 K 3:11-14	II, 175
2. Ws 7:7-10, 15-16	VII, 156
3. Si 15:1-6	—
4. Si 39:6-11	—

b) In Eastertime:

1. Ac 2:14a, 22-24, 32-36	IV, 61 and 113
2. Ac 13:26-33	IV, 149

Second Reading

1. 1 Co 1:18-25	VI, 330
2. 1 Co 2:1-10a	II, 180 and 239
3. 1 Co 2:10b-16	VIII, 7
4. Ep 3:8-12	IV, 362
5. Ep 4:1-7, 11-13	VIII, 197 and 201
6. 2 Tm 1:13-14; 2:1-3	VII, 135
7. 2 Tm 4:1-5	VI, 24

Gospel

1. Mt 5:13-16	II, 185
2. Mt 23:8-12	III, 95
3. Mk 4:1-10, 13-20	II, 110

F. COMMON OF VIRGINS

First Reading

a) Outside of Eastertime:

1. Sg 8:6-7	—
2. Ho 2:14b, 15c, 19-20	VI, 130

b) In Eastertime:

1. Rv 19:1, 5-9a	—
2. Rv 21:1-5a	IV, 162

Second Reading

1. 1 Co 7:25-35	VIII, 38
2. 2 Co 10:17-11:2	VI, 79

Gospel

1. Mt 19:3-12	VI, 281
2. Mt 25:1-13	VII, 255
3. Lk 10:38-42	V, 203

G. COMMON OF SAINTS

(R)—for Religious
(W)—for Widows
(T)—for Teachers
(M)—For those who work for the disadvantaged

First Reading

a) Outside of Eastertime:

1. Gn 12:1-4a	III, 62
2. Lv 19:1-2, 17-18	II, 288
3. Dt 6:3-9	VI, 255
4. Dt 10:8-9 (R)	—
5. 1 K 19:4-9a, 11-15a (R)	VI, 47
6. 1 K 19:16b, 19-21 (R)	V, 112
7. Tb 8:4-9 (vulgate)	—
8. Tb 12:6-13 (vulgate) (M)	VI, 24
9. Jdt 8:2-8 (W)	—
10. Est 13:8-14, 17	—
11. Pr 31:10-13, 19-20, 30-31	VII, 273
12. Si 2:7-11	II, 310
13. Si 3:17-24	VII, 3
14. Si 26:1-4, 13-16	—
15. Is 58:6-11 (M)	II, 177
16. Jr 20:7-9	VII, 1
17. Mi 6:6-8	VI, 190
18. Zp 2:3; 3:12-13	II, 128

b) In Eastertime:

1. Ac 4:32-35 (R)	IV, 22
2. Rv 3:14b, 20-22	VIII, 284
3. Rv 19:1, 5-9a	—
4. Rv 21:5-7	—

Second Reading

1. Rm 8:26-30	VIII, 214
2. 1 Co 1:26-31	II, 131
3. 1 Co 12:31—13:13	II, 135
4. 2 Co 10:17—11:2	VI, 79
5. Ga 2:19-20	V, 64
6. Ga 6:14-16	V, 145
7. Ep 3:14-19	VIII, 192
8. Ep 6:10-13, 18	VIII, 222
9. Ph 3:8-14	III, 212
10. Ph 4:4-9	I, 95
11. 1 Tm 5:3-10 (W)	—
12. Jm 2:14-17	VII, 59
13. 1 P 3:1-9	—
14. 1 P 4:7b-11	II, 371
15. 1 Jn 3:14-18 (M)	I, 275
16. 1 Jn 4:7-16	IV, 362
17. 1 Jn 5:1-5	IV, 28

Gospel

1.	Mt 5:1-12a	II, 137
2.	Mt 5:13-16	II, 185
3.	Mt 11:25-30	IV, 366
4.	Mt 13:44-46	VI, 221
5.	Mt 16:24-27	VI, 253
6.	Mt 18:1-4	VI, 266
7.	Mt 19:3-12 (R)	VI, 281
8.	Mt 25:1-13	VII, 255
9.	Mt 25:14-30	VII, 278
10.	Mt 25:31-46	VII, 303
11.	Mk 3:31-35	II, 107
12.	Mk 9:34-37 (T)	VII, 89
13.	Mk 10:13-16 (T)	II, 327
14.	Mk 10:17-30 (R)	VII, 164
15.	Lk 9:57-62 (R)	VIII, 110
16.	Lk 10:38-42	V, 203
17.	Lk 12:32-34 (R)	V, 280
18.	Lk 12:35-40	V, 280
19.	Lk 14:25-33 (R)	VII, 41
20.	Jn 15:1-8	IV, 168
21.	Jn 15:9-17	IV, 203
22.	Jn 17:20-26	IV, 263

IV. THE LECTIONARY OF VOTIVE MASSES

A. TRIUMPH OF THE HOLY CROSS

First Reading

a) Outside of Eastertime:

1.	Ex 12:1-8, 11-14	III, 285
2.	Ws 2:1a, 12-22	III, 201
3.	Is 50:4-9a	III, 275
4.	Is 52:13-53:12	VII, 182
5.	Zc 12:10-11; 13:6-7	—

b) In Eastertime:

1.	Ac 10:34-43	III, 331
2.	Ac 13:26-33	IV, 149
3.	Rv 1:5-8	III, 281
4.	Rv 5:6-12	VIII, 292

Second Reading

1.	1 Co 1:18-25	VI, 330
2.	Ep 2:13-18	V, 198
3.	Ph 2:6-11	III, 250
4.	Ph 3:8-14	III, 212
5.	Heb 5:7-9	III, 211

Gospel

1.	Mk 8:31-34	II, 276
2.	Mk 12:1-12	VI, 3
3.	Lk 24:35-48	IV, 79
4.	Jn 12:31-36a	III, 217

B. HOLY EUCHARIST

First Reading

a) Outside of Eastertime:

1.	Gn 14:18-20	IV, 337
2.	Ex 16:2-4, 12-15	V, 246
3.	Ex 24:3-8	IV, 336
4.	Dt 8:2-3, 14b-16a	IV, 335
5.	1 K 19:4-8	V, 269
6.	Pr 9:1-6	V, 297

b) In Eastertime:

1.	Ac 2:42-47	IV, 22
2.	Ac 10:34a, 37-43	III, 331

Second Reading

1.	1 Co 10:16-17	IV, 339
2.	1 Co 11:23-26	III, 288
3.	Heb 9:11-15	IV, 340

Gospel

1.	Mk 14:12-16, 22-26	IV, 345
2.	Lk 9:11b-17	IV, 346
3.	Lk 24:13-35	III, 336
4.	Jn 6:1-15	IV, 57
5.	Jn 6:24-35	V, 254
6.	Jn 6:41-51a	V, 278
7.	Jn 6:51-58	IV, 344
8.	Jn 21:1-14	IV, 13

C. SACRED HEART

First Reading

a) Outside of Eastertime:

1.	Ex 34:4b-6, 8-9	IV, 314
2.	Dt 7:6-11	IV, 358
3.	Dt 10:12-22	VI, 261
4.	Is 49:13-15	II, 328
5.	Jr 31:1-4	VI, 245
6.	Ez 34:11-16	IV, 360
7.	Ho 11:1, 3-4, 8e-9	IV, 359

b) In Eastertime:

1.	Rv 3:14b, 20-22	VIII, 284
2.	Rv 5:6-12	VIII, 292

Second Reading

1.	Rm 5:5-11	IV, 364
2.	Ep 1:3-10	VIII, 166
3.	Ep 3:8-12	IV, 362
4.	Ep 3:14-19	VIII, 192

5. Ph 1:8-11	I, 58
6. 1 Jn 4:7-16	IV, 362

Gospel

1. Mt 11:25-30	IV, 366
2. Lk 15:1-10	VIII, 246
3. Lk 15:1-3, 11-32	III, 177
4. Jn 10:11-18	IV, 123
5. Jn 15:1-8	IV, 168
6. Jn 15:9-17	IV, 203
7. Jn 17:20-26	IV, 263
8. Jn 19:31-37	IV, 369

D. PRECIOUS BLOOD

First Reading

a) Outside of Eastertime:

1. Ex 12:21-27	VI, 181
2. Ex 24:3-8	IV, 336

b) In Eastertime:

1. Rv 1:5-8	III, 281
2. Rv 7:9-14	IV, 119

Second Reading

1. Heb 9:11-15	IV, 340
2. Heb 12:18-19, 22-24	VII, 8
3. 1 P 1:17-21	IV, 71
4. 1 Jn 5:4-8	I, 294

Gospel

1. Mk 14:12-16, 22-26	IV, 345
2. Mk 15:16-20	—
3. Lk 22:39-44	—
4. Jn 19:31-37	IV, 369

E. HOLY NAME

First Reading

a) Outside of Eastertime:

1. Ex 3:13-15	III, 115
2. Si 51:8-12	—

b) In Eastertime:

1. Ac 3:1-10	IV, 4
2. Ac 4:8-12	IV, 114
3. Ac 5:27b-32, 40b-42	IV, 68

Second Reading

1. 1 Co 1:1-3	II, 24
2. Ph 2:6-11	III, 250
3. Col 3:12-17	VIII, 42

Gospel

1. Mt 1:18-25	I, 140
2. Lk 2:16-21	I, 244
3. Jn 14:6-14	IV, 152

F. HOLY SPIRIT

Readings for Pentecost may be used,	IV, 291-301
or those for Confirmation	IX, 135

G. ALL OR ONE OF THE APOSTLES

First Reading

Ep 2:19-22	VIII, 185

Gospel

Lk 6:12-16	VIII, 34

V. THE LECTIONARY OF MASSES FOR VARIOUS OCCASIONS

A. FOR VOCATIONS OF PRIESTS AND RELIGIOUS

Old Testament Reading

1. Gn 12:1-4a — III, 62
2. Ex 3:1-6, 9-12 — VI, 164
3. 1 S 3:1-10 — II, 7
4. 1 K 19:16b, 19-21 — V, 112
5. Is 6:1-8 — —
6. Jr 1:4-9 — VI, 198
7. Jr 20:7-9 — VII, 1

New Testament Reading

1. 2 Co 5:14-20 — VI, 50
2. Ph 3:8-14 — III, 212
3. Heb 5:1-10 — II, 48

Gospel

1. Mt 9:35-38 — VI, 139
2. Mk 10:17-27 — II, 349
3. Mk 10:28-30 — II, 356
4. Lk 5:1-11 — II, 188
5. Lk 9:57-62 — VIII, 110
6. Lk 14:25-33 — VII, 41
7. Jn 1:35-51 — I, 273 and 277
8. Jn 15:9-17 — IV, 203

B. FOR UNITY OF CHRISTIANS

Old Testament Reading

1. Dt 30:1-4 — —
2. Ez 36:23-28 — VI, 296
3. Ez 37:15-19, 21b-22, 26-28 — III, 245
4. Zp 3:16b-20 — I, 92

New Testament Reading

1. 1 Co 1:10-13 — II, 76
2. Ep 2:19-22 — VIII, 185
3. Ep 4:1-6 — V, 221
4. Ep 4:30-5:2 — V, 273
5. Ph 2:1-13 — VII, 106
6. Col 3:9b-17 — I, 204 and V, 251
7. 1 Tm 2:5-8 — VII, 85
8. 1 Jn 4:9-15 — IV, 362

Gospel

1. Mt 18:19-22 — VI, 275
2. Lk 9:49-55 — VIII, 107
3. Jn 10:11-16 — IV, 123
4. Jn 11:45-52 — III, 246
5. Jn 13:1-15 — III, 290
6. Jn 17:1-11a — IV, 259
7. Jn 17:11b-19 — IV, 261
8. Jn 17:20-26 — IV, 263

C. FOR THE SPREAD OF THE GOSPEL

Old Testament Reading

1. Is 2:1-5 — I, 1
2. Is 56:1, 6-7 — V, 296
3. Is 60:1-6 — I, 252
4. Jon 3:10-4:11 — VIII, 127
5. Zc 8:20-23 — V, 141

New Testament Reading

1. Ac 1:3-8 — IV, 228
2. Ac 11:19-26 — IV, 141
3. Ac 13:46-49 — IV, 152
4. Rm 10:9-18 — III, 19
5. Ep 3:2-12 — VIII, 189
6. 1 Tm 2:1-8 — VII, 85

Gospel

1. Mt 28:16-20 — IV, 232
2. Mk 16:15-20 — IV, 234
3. Lk 24:44-53 — IV, 238
4. Jn 11:45-52 — III, 246
5. Jn 17:11b, 17-23 — IV, 261 and 263

D. FOR PERSECUTED CHRISTIANS

Old Testament Reading

1. Est 13:8-11, 15-17	—
2. 1 M 2:49-52, 57-64	—
3. Is 41:8-10, 13-14	—
4. Dn 3:2, 11-20	III, 237

New Testament Reading

1. Ac 4:1-5, 18-21	IV, 11 and 17
2. Ac 4:23-31	IV, 48
3. Ac 5:27b-32, 40b-42	IV, 68
4. Ph 1:27-30	—
5. Heb 12:2-13	V, 302 and 328
6. 1 P 1:3-9	II, 347
7. Rv 7:9-10, 14b-17	IV, 119

Gospel

1. Mt 5:1-12a	II, 137
2. Mt 10:17-22	I, 224
3. Mt 10:26-33	V, 95
4. Jn 15:18-21, 26-16:4	IV, 194 and 221
5. Jn 17:11b-19	IV, 261

E. FOR PEACE AND JUSTICE

Old Testament Reading

1. Is 9:2-7	I, 178
2. Is 32:15-20	—
3. Is 57:15-19	—

New Testament Reading

1. Ph 4:6-9	VII, 133
2. Col 3:12-15	VIII, 42
3. Jm 3:13-18	II, 307

Gospel

1. Mt 5:1-12a	II, 137
2. Mt 5:38-48	II, 296
3. Jn 14:23-29	IV, 204
4. Jn 20:19-23	IV, 301

F. IN TIME OF WAR AND CIVIL DISTURBANCES

Old Testament Reading

1. Gn 4:3-10	—
2. Mi 4:1-4	—
3. Zc 9:9-10	V, 141

New Testament Reading

1. Ga 5:17-26	VIII, 161
2. Ep 4:30-5:2	V, 273
3. Jm 4:1-10	II, 311

Gospel

1. Mt 5:20-24	III, 54
2. Jn 15:9-12	IV, 203

Readings for Peace and Justice Mass may be used.

G. BLESSING OF MAN'S LABOR

Old Testament Reading

1. Gn 1:26-2:3	II, 207
2. Gn 2:4b-9, 15	II, 213

New Testament Reading

2 Th 3:6-12, 16	VII, 277

Gospel

1. Mt 6:31-34	II, 335
2. Mt 25:14-30	VI, 336

H. FOR THOSE SUFFERING FROM FAMINE OR HUNGER

Old Testament Reading

1. Dt 24:17-22	—
2. Jb 31:16-20, 24-25, 31-32	—
3. Is 58:6-11	II, 177

New Testament Reading

1. Ac 11:27-30	—

2. 2 Co 8:1-5, 9-15	V, 116
3. 2 Co 9:6-15	VI, 61

Gospel

1. Mt 25:31-46	III, 41
2. Mk 6:34-44	I, 284
3. Lk 14:12-14	VII, 16
4. Lk 16:19-31	III, 102

I. FOR REFUGEES AND EXILES

Old Testament Reading

1. Dt 10:17-19	VI, 261
2. Dt 24:17-22	—

New Testament Reading

1. Rm 12:9-16b	VIII, 237
2. Heb 11:13-16	V, 275
3. Heb 13:1-3, 14-16	II, 170

Gospel

1. Mt 2:13-15, 19-23	I, 206
2. Lk 10:25-37	V, 177

J. FOR THE SICK

Old Testament Reading

1. 2 K 20:1-6	—
2. Is 53:1-5, 10-11	VII, 182

New Testament Reading

1. Ac 28:7-10	—
2. 2 Co 4:10-18	V, 37
3. 2 Co 12:7b-10	V, 144
4. Jm 5:13-16	II, 324

Gospel

1. Mt 8:14-17	VI, 102
2. Mk 16:15-20	IV, 234
3. Lk 22:39-44	—
4. Jn 15:1-8	IV, 168

K. IN THANKSGIVING

Old Testament Reading

1. 1 K 8:55-61	—
2. Si 50:22-24	—
3. Is 63:7-9	—
4. Zp 3:14-15	I, 92

New Testament Reading

1. 1 Co 1:3-9	I, 8
2. Ep 1:3-14	V, 170
3. Col 3:12-17	VIII, 42

Gospel

1. Mk 5:18-20	II, 156
2. Lk 17:11-19	VIII, 264

VI. LECTIONARY OF RITUAL MASSES

A. THE PREPARATION AND BAPTISM OF ADULTS

Beginning of the Catechumenate
First Reading

Gn 12:1-4a	III, 62

Gospel

Jn 1:35-42	I, 273

Election
Taken from the first Sunday of Lent.

First Scrutiny
Taken from the third Sunday of Lent

Second Scrutiny
Taken from the fourth Sunday of Lent.

Third Scrutiny
Taken from the fifth Sunday of Lent.

Presentation of the Creed
First Reading

Dt 6:1-7	VII, 228

Second Reading

Rm 10:8-13	III, 19
1 Co 15:1-8a	II, 183

Gospel

Mt 16:13-18	V, 329
Jn 12:44-50	IV, 145

Presentation of the Lord's Prayer
First Reading

Ho 11:1, 3-4, 8e-9	IV, 359

Second Reading

Rm 8:14-17, 26-27	IV, 319 and V, 196
Ga 4:4-7	I, 241

Gospel

Lk 11:1-2a	VIII, 134
Mt 6:9b-13	III, 44

Rites of Immediate Preparation
Gospel

Mk 7:31-37	II, 226

Baptism During the Easter Vigil
Obligatory Readings

Ex 14:15-15:1	III, 319
Is 55:1-11	III, 322
Ez 36:16-28	VI, 296

B. CHRISTIAN INITIATION APART FROM THE EASTER VIGIL

Old Testament Reading

1. Gn 15:1-6, 18a	VI, 86
2. Gn 17:1-8	III, 241
3. Gn 35:1-4, 6-7a	—
4. Dt 30:15-20	III, 3
5. Jos 24:1-2a, 15-17, 18b-25a	V, 321
6. 2 K 5:9-15a	III, 143
7. Is 44:1-3	VI, 186
8. Jr 31:31-34	III, 208
9. Ez 36:24-28	VI, 296

Or the Old Testament readings for the Easter Vigil.

New Testament Reading

1. Ac 2:14a, 36-40a, 41-42	IV, 113
2. Ac 8:26-38	IV, 102
3. Rm 6:3-11	III, 325
4. Rm 8:28-32, 35, 37-39	V, 220 and 248
5. 1 Co 12:12-13	IV, 299
6. Ga 3:26-28	V, 93
7. Ep 1:3-10, 13-14	V, 170
8. Ep 4:1-6	V, 221
9. Col 3:9b-17	VIII, 42
10. Tt 3:4-7	VIII, 263
11. Heb 10:22-25	II, 113

12. 1 P 2:4-5, 9-10 — II, 366
13. Rv 19:1, 5-9a — —

Gospel

1. Mt 16:24-27 — VI, 253
2. Mt 28:18-20 — IV, 232
3. Mk 1:9-11 — I, 307
4. Mk 10:13-16 — II, 327
5. Mk 16:15-16, 19-20 — IV, 234
6. Lk 24:44-53 — IV, 238
7. Jn 1:1-5, 9-14, 16-18 — I, 189
8. Jn 1:29-34 — I, 271
9. Jn 3:1-6 — IV, 50
10. Jn 3:16-21 — IV, 55
11. Jn 12:44-50 — IV, 145
12. Jn 15:1-11 — IV, 168 and 191

C. BAPTISM OF CHILDREN

Old Testament Reading

1. Ex 17:3-7 — III, 110
2. Ez 36:24-28 — VI, 296
3. Ez 47:1-9, 12 — III, 193

New Testament Reading

1. Rm 6:3-5 — III, 325
2. Rm 8:28-32 — V, 220
3. 1 Co 12:12-13 — VIII, 60
4. Ga 3:26-28 — V, 93
5. Ep 4:1-6 — V, 221
6. 1 P 2:4-5, 9-10 — II, 366

Gospel

1. Mt 22:35-40 — VI, 303
2. Mt 28:18-20 — IV, 232
3. Mk 1:9-11 — I, 307
4. Mk 10:13-16 — II, 327
5. Mk 12:28b-34 — III, 158
6. Jn 3:1-6 — IV, 50
7. Jn 4:5-14 — III, 123
8. Jn 6:44-47 — IV, 104
9. Jn 7:37b-39a — IV, 294
10. Jn 9:1-7 — III, 171
11. Jn 15:1-11 — IV, 168 and 191
12. Jn 19:31-35 — IV, 369

D. CONFIRMATION

Old Testament Reading

1. Is 11:1-4b — I, 47
2. Is 42:1-3 — I, 301
3. Is 61:1-3d, 6ab, 8c-9 — III, 280
4. Ez 36:24-28 — IV, 291
5. Jl 2:23ab, 26-30a — —

New Testament Reading

1. Ac 1:3-8 — IV, 228
2. Ac 2:1-6, 14, 22b-23, 32-33 — IV, 1 and 295
3. Ac 8:1, 4, 14-17 — IV, 195
4. Ac 10:1, 33-34a, 37-44 — III, 331
5. Ac 19:1b-6a — IV, 279
6. Rm 5:1-2, 5-8 — IV, 321 and 364
7. Rm 8:14-17 — IV, 319
8. Rm 8:26-27 — V, 196
9. 1 Co 12:4-13 — IV, 299
10. Ga 5:16-17, 22-23a, 24-25 — VIII, 161
11. Ep 1:3a, 4a, 13-19a — I, 279
12. Ep 4:1-6 — V, 221

Gospel

1. Mt 5:1-12a — II, 137
2. Mt 16:24-27 — VI, 253
3. Mt 25:14-30 — VI, 336
4. Mk 1:9-11 — I, 307
5. Lk 4:16-22a — I, 291
6. Lk 8:4-10a, 11b-15 — VIII, 80
7. Lk 10:21-24 — I, 32
8. Jn 7:37b-39 — IV, 294
9. Jn 14:15-17 — IV, 201
10. Jn 14:23-26 — IV, 204
11. Jn 15:18-21, 26-27 — IV, 194
12. Jn 16:5-7, 12-13a — IV, 223 and 326

E. MARRIAGE

Old Testament Reading

1. Gn 1:26-28, 31a —
2. Gn 2:18-24 VII, 130
3. Gn 24:48-51, 58-67 —
4. Tb 7:11b-15 (vulgate) VI, 14
5. Tb 8:4-9a (vulgate) VI, 14
6, Sg 2:8-10, 14, 16a; 8:6-7ab I, 166
7. Si 26:1-4, 13-16 —
8. Jr 31:31-32a, 33-34a III, 208

New Testament Reading

1. Rm 8:31b-35, 37-39 VIII, 220
2. Rm 12:1-2, 9-18 VII, 4 and VIII, 237
3. 1 Co 6:13c-15a, 17-20 II, 25
4. 1 Co 12:31-13:8a II, 135
5. Ep 5:2a, 21-33 VIII, 210
6. Col 3:12-17 VIII, 42
7. 1 P 3:1-9 —
8. 1 Jn 3:18-24 IV, 161
9. 1 Jn 4:7-12 IV, 257
10. Rv 19:1, 5-9a VIII, 312

Gospel

1. Mt 5:1-12a II, 137
2. Mt 5:13-16 II, 185
3. Mt 7:21, 24-29 I, 39
4. Mt 19:3-6 VI, 281
5. Mt 22:35-40 VI, 303
6. Mk 10:6-9 VII, 138
7. Jn 2:1-11 II, 34
8. Jn 15:9-12 IV, 203
9. Jn 15:12-16 IV, 191
10. Jn 17-20-26 IV, 263

F. MASSES FOR THE DEAD

Old Testament Reading

1. Jb 19:1, 23-27b VIII, 112
2. Ws 3:1-9c —
3. Ws 4:7-15 —
4. Is 25:6a, 7-9 I, 34
5. Lm 3:17-26 —
6. Dn 12:1-3 VII, 273
7. 2 M 12:43-45 —

New Testament Reading

1. Ac 10:34-43 I, 302
2. Rm 5:5-11 IV, 364
3. Rm 5:17-21 VIII, 182
4. Rm 6:3-9 III, 325
5. Rm 8:14-23 IV, 319 and V, 169
6. Rm 8:31b-35, 37-39 VIII, 220
7. Rm 14:7-9, 10b-12 VII, 58
8. 1 Co 15:20-24a, 25-28 VII, 299
9. 1 Co 15:51-57 II, 334
10. 2 Co 5:1, 6-10 V, 63
11. Ph 3:20-21 III, 71
12. 1 Th 4:13-18 VII, 252
13. 2 Tm 2:8-13 VII, 159
14. 1 Jn 3:1-2 I, 270
15. 1 Jn 3:14-16 I, 275
16. Rv 14:13 —
17. Rv 20:11-21:2 VIII, 315
18. Rv 21:1-5a, 6b-7 —

Gospel

1. Mt 5:1-12a II, 137
2. Mt 11:25-30 IV, 366
3. Mt 25:1-13 VI, 332
4. Mt 25:31-46 III, 41
5. Mk 15:33-39; 16:1-6 III, 255 and 329
6. Lk 7:11-17 V, 43
7. Lk 12:35-40 V, 280
8. Lk 23:33, 39-43 VII, 307
9. Lk 23:44-49; 24:1-5 —
10. Lk 24:13-35 III, 336
11. Jn 6:37-40 IV, 101
12. Jn 6:51-58 IV, 344
13. Jn 11:17-27 III, 215
14. Jn 11:32-45 III, 215
15. Jn 12:23-28 III, 217
16. Jn 14:1-6 IV, 152
17. Jn 17:24-26 IV, 263

G. BURIAL OF BAPTIZED CHILDREN

Old Testament Reading

1. Is 25:6a, 7-9	I, 34
2. Lm 3:17-26	—

New Testament Reading

1. Rm 6:3-4, 8-9	V, 114
2. Rm 14:7-9	VII, 58
3. 1 Co 15:20-23	VII, 299
4. Ep 1:3-5	I, 279
5. 1 Th 4:13-14, 18	VII, 252
6. Rv 7:9-10, 15-17	IV, 119
7. Rv 21:1a, 3-5a	IV, 162

Gospel

1. Mt 11:25-30	IV, 366
2. Jn 6:37-40	—
3. Jn 6:51-58	IV, 344
4. Jn 11:32-38, 40	III, 215

H. BURIAL OF NON-BAPTIZED CHILDREN

First Reading

1. Is 25:6a, 7-8a	I, 34
2. Lm 3:17-26	—

Gospel

Mk 15:33-46	—

In the following calendar, solemnities are designated by boldface capital letters; feasts by boldface lowercase letters.

The boldface initials refer to the various "commons":

C—Dedication of a Church
B.V.M.—Common of the Blessed Virgin Mary
M—Common of Martyrs
P—Common of Pastors
  P (m)—for missionaries
  P (p)—for popes
D—Common of doctors
V—Common of virgins
S—Common of saints
  S (r)—for religious
  S (w)—for widows
  S (e)—for educators
  S (m)—for those who perform works of mercy

The mention of a scriptural reading in parentheses indicates a preference for that reading to the corresponding "common".

When there is no parenthesis, the mention of a biblical reading indicates a new suggestion relating to the reading of the "common".

VII. THE LECTIONARY OF SAINTS

JANUARY

Day	Celebration		Readings	Reference
1.	**SOLEMNITY OF MARY, MOTHER OF GOD**			I, 241
	Octave of Christmas			
2.	Basil the Great and Gregory Nazianzen			**P** or **D**
	bishops and doctors			
7.	Raymond of Penyafort		(2 Co 5:14-20)	**P**
	priest			
13.	Hilary			**P** or **D**
	bishop and doctor		1 Jn 2:18-25	I, 236
17.	Anthony			**S (r)**
	abbot		Mt 19:16-26	VI, 288, 290
20.	Fabian			**M** or **P**
	pope and martyr			
	Sebastian			**M**
	martyr			
21.	Agnes			**M** or **V**
	virgin and martyr			
22.	Vincent			**M**
	deacon and martyr			
24.	Francis de Sales			**P** or **D**
	bishop and doctor			
15.	**Conversion of Paul**		(I) Ac 22:3-16	—
	apostle		Ac 9:1-22	IV, 106
			(G) Mc 16:15-18	IV, 234
26.	Timothy and Titus			**P**
	bishops	except	(I) 2 Tm 1:1-8	VI, 9
			or Tt 1:1-5	VIII, 257
27.	Angela Merici			**V** or **S (e)**
	virgin			
28.	Thomas Aquinas			**D** or **P**
	priest and doctor			
31.	John Bosco			**P** or **S (e)**
	priest			

FEBRUARY

Day	Celebration	Reference
2.	**Presentation of Jesus**	IX, 1
3.	Blaise	**M** or **P**
	bishop and martyr	
	Ansgar	**P (m)**
	bishop	

5. Agatha *virgin and martyr*		**M** or **V**
6. Paul Miki and companions *martyrs*	Ga 2:19-20 Mt 28:16-20	**M** V, 64 IV, 232
8. Jerome Emiliani *priest*		**S (e)**
10. Scholastica *virgin*		**V** or **S (r)**
11. Our Lady of Lourdes	Is 66:10-14c	**B.V.M.** V, 142
14. Cyril, *monk* and Methodius, *bishop*		**P (m)** or **S**
17. Seven Founders of the Order of Servites		**S (r)**
21. Peter Damian *bishop and doctor*		**D** or **P** or **S (r)**
22. **Chair of Peter** *apostle*	(I) 1 P 5:1-4 (G) Mt 16:13-19	— V, 329
23. Polycarp *bishop and martyr*	Rv 2:8-11	—

MARCH

4. Casimir	**S**
7. Perpetua and Felicity *martyrs*	**M**
8. John of God *religious*	**S (r or m)**
9. Frances of Rome *religious*	**S**
17. Patrick *bishop*	**P (m)**
18. Cyril of Jerusalem *bishop and doctor*	**P or D**
19. **JOSEPH, HUSBAND OF MARY**	IX, 11
23. Turibius of Mongrovejo *bishop*	**P**
25. **ANNUNCIATION**	IX, 23

APRIL

2. Francis of Paola *hermit*	**S (r)**
4. Isidore *bishop and doctor*	**P or D**

5. Vincent Ferrer *priest*		**P (m)**
7. John Baptist de la Salle *priest*		**P** or **S (e)**
11. Stanislaus *bishop and martyr*		**M** or **P**
13. Martin I *pope and martyr*		**M** or **P (p)**
21. Anselm *bishop and doctor*		**P** or **D**
23. George *martyr*		**M**
24. Fidelis of Sigmaringen *priest and martyr*		**M** or **P**
25. **Mark** *evangelist*	(I) 1 P 5:5b-14 (G) Mc 16:15-20	— IV, 234
28. Peter Chanel *priest and martyr*		**M** or **P (m)**
29. Catherine of Siena *virgin and doctor*		**D** or **V**
30. Pius V *pope*		**P (p)**

MAY

1. Joseph the Worker	(I) Gn 1:26-2:3 Col 3:14-15, 17, 23-24 (G) Mt 13:54-58	II, 207 I, 204 VI, 228
2. Athanasius *bishop and doctor*	 1 Jn 5:1-5 Mt 10:22-25a	**P** or **D** IV, 28 VI, 150, 155
3. **Philip and James** *apostles*	(I) 1 Co 15:1-8 (G) Jn 14:6-14	II, 183 IV, 152
12. Nereus and Acilleus *martyrs*		**M**
Pancras *martyr*		**M**
14. **Matthias** *apostle*	(I) Ac 1:15-17, 20-26 (G) Jn 15:9-17	IV, 252 IV, 203
18. John I *pope and martyr*		**M** or **P (p)**
20. Bernadine of Siena *priest*	 Ac 4:8-12	**P (m)** IV, 114

25. Venerable Bede *priest and doctor*		**P** or **D**
Gregory VII *pope*		**P (p)**
Mary Magdalene de Pazzi *virgin*		**V** or **S (r)**
26. Philip Neri *priest*		**P** or **S (r)**
27. Augustine of Canterbury *bishop*		**P (m)**
31. **Visitation**	(I) Zp 3:14-18a Rm 12:9-16b (G) Lk 1:39-56	I, 92 VIII, 237 I, 146
Saturday following the second Sunday after Pentecost— Immaculate Heart of Mary		**B.V.M.**
except	Lk 2:41-51	I, 209

JUNE

1. Justin *martyr*	 1 Co 1:18-25	**M** VI, 330
2. Marcellinus and Peter *martyrs*		**M**
3. Charles Lwanga and companions *martyrs*		**M**
5. Boniface *bishop and martyr*		**M** or **P (m)**
6. Norbert *bishop*		**P** or **S (r)**
9. Ephrem *deacon and doctor*		**D**
11. Barnabas *apostle*	(I) Ac 11:21b-26; 13:1-3 (G) Mt 10:7-13	 IV, 141-144 VI, 145
13. Anthony of Padua *priest and doctor*		**P** or **D** or **S (r)**
19. Romuald *abbot*		**S (r)**
21. Aloysius Gonzaga *religious*		**S (r)**
22. Paulinus of Nola *bishop*	 2 Co 8:9-15	**P** V, 116
John Fisher *bishop and martyr* and Thomas More *martyr*		**M**

24. **BIRTH OF JOHN THE BAPTIST**		IX, 29
27. Cyril of Alexandria *bishop and doctor*		**P** or **D**
28. Irenaeus *bishop and martyr*		**M** or **D**
29. **PETER AND PAUL** *apostles*		IX, 41
30. First Martyrs of the Church of Rome	(Rm 8:31b-39)	**M**
	Mt 24:4-13	VI, 338

JULY

3. **Thomas** *apostle*	(I) Ep 2:19-22	VIII, 185
	(G) Jn 20:24-29	IV, 30
4. Elizabeth of Portugal		**S (m)**
5. Anthony Zaccaria *priest*		**P** or **S (e or r)**
6. Maria Goretti *virgin and martyr*	1 Co 6:13c-15a, 17-20	II, 25
11. Benedict *abbot*	Pr 2:1-9	**S (r)**
13. Henry		**S**
14. Camillus de Lellis *priest*		**S (m)**
15. Bonaventure *bishop and doctor*		—
16. Our Lady of Mount Carmel		**B.V.M.**
21. Lawrence of Brindisi *priest and doctor*		**P** or **D**
22. Mary Magdalene	(I) Ct 3:1-4a	—
	2 Co 5:14-17	V, 92
	(G) Jn 20:1-2, 11-18	IV, 2
23. Bridget *religious*		**S (r)**
25. **James** *apostle*	(I) 2 Co 4:7-15	VI, 45
	(G) Mt 20:20-28	III, 98
26. Joachim and Ann *parents of Mary*	(I) Si 44:1, 10-15	II, 370
	(G) Mt 13:16-17	VI, 203
29. Martha		**S**
except	Jn 11:19-27	III, 215
or	Lk 10:38-42	V, 203
30. Peter Chrysologus *bishop and doctor*		**P** or **D**
31. Ignatius of Loyola *priest*	1 Co 10:31-11:1	**P** or **S (r)** II, 240

AUGUST

Feast	Readings	
1. Alphonsus Liguori *bishop and doctor*	Rm 8:1-4	**P** or **D** VIII, 199
2. Eusebius of Vercelli *bishop*		**P**
4. John Vianney *priest*	(Ez 3:16-21) Mt 9:35-10:1	**P** I, 44
5. Dedication of Saint Mary Major		**B.V.M.**
6. **Transfiguration**		IX, 55
7. Sixtus II *pope and martyr* and companions *martyrs* Cajetan *priest*		**M** **P** or **S (r)**
8. Dominic *priest*		**P (m)** or **S (r)**
10. **Lawrence** *deacon and martyr*	(I) 2 Co 9:6-10 (G) Jn 12:24-26	VI, 61 III, 217
11. Clare *virgin*		**S (r)**
13. Pontian, *pope and martyr* and Hippolytus, *priest and martyr*		 **M** or **P**
15. **ASSUMPTION**		IX, 60
16. Stephen of Hungary		**S**
19. John Eudes *priest*	(Ep 3:14-19)	**P** or **S**
20. Bernard *abbot and doctor*		**D** or **S (r)**
21. Pius X *pope*	(1 Th 2:2b-8)	**P (p)**
22. Queenship of Mary	(Is 9:2-7; Lk 1:39-47)	**B.V.M.**
23. Rose of Lima *virgin*		**V** or **S (r)**
24. **Bartholomew** *apostle*	(I) Rv 21:9b-14 (G) Jn 1:45-51	IV, 200 I, 277
25. Louis Joseph Calasanz *priest*		**S** **P** or **S (e)**
27. Monica	(Si 26:1-4, 16-21) Lk 7:11-17	**S** V, 43

28. Augustine		**P** or **D**
bishop and doctor	1 Jn 4:7-16	IV, 362
	Mt 23:8-12	III, 95
29. Beheading of John the Baptist	(I) Jr 1:17-19	II, 130
martyr	(G) Mk 6:17-29	II, 173

SEPTEMBER

3. Gregory the Great		**P (p)** or **D**
pope and doctor		
8. **Birth of Mary**	(I) Mi 5:1-4a	I, 134
	Rm 8:28-30	V, 220
	(G) Mt 1:1-16, 18-23	I, 178
13. John Chrysostom		**P** or **D**
bishop and doctor		
14. **Exaltation of the Holy Cross**		IX, 74
15. Our Lady of Sorrows	(I) Heb 5:7-9	III, 211
	(G) Jn 19:25-27	—
	Lk 2:33-35	I, 233
16. Cornelius		
pope and martyr		
and Cyprian		**M** or **P**
bishop and martyr		
17. Robert Bellarmine		**P** or **D**
bishop and doctor		
19. Januarius		**M** or **P**
bishop and martyr		
21. **Matthew**	(I) Ep 4:1-7, 11-13	VIII, 197, 201
apostle and evangelist	(G) Mt 9:9-13	V, 40
26. Cosmas and Damian		**M**
martyrs		
27. Vincent de Paul	(1 Co 1:26-31)	**P (m)**
priest		or **S (m)**
28. Wenceslaus		**M**
martyr		
29. **Michael, Gabriel and Raphael**	(I) Dn 7:9-10, 13-14	VIII, 314
archangels	Rv 12:7-12a	—
	(G) Jn 1:47-51	I, 277
30. Jerome		**D** or **P**
priest and doctor	2 Tm 3:14-17	VI, 20

OCTOBER

1. Theresa of the Child Jesus		**V** or **S (r)**
virgin	Is 66:10-14c	V, 142
	Mt 18:1-4	VI, 266

2. Guardian Angels	(I) Ex 23:20-23	—
	(G) Mt 18:1-5, 10	VI, 266
4. Francis of Assisi		**S (r)**
	(I) Ga 6:14-18	V, 145
	(G) Mt 11:25-30	IV, 366
6. Bruno *priest*		**P** or **S (r)**
7. Our Lady of the Rosary	(Lk 1:26-38)	**B.V.M.**
9. Denis *bishop and martyr* and companions *martyrs*		**M**
John Leonardi *priest*		**P** or **S (m)**
14. Callistus I *pope and martyr*		**M** or **P (p)**
15. Theresa of Avila *virgin and doctor*		**D** or **V** or **S (r)**
	Rm 8:22-27	IV, 292
16. Hedwig *religious*		**S (r)**
Margaret Mary Alacoque *virgin*	(Ep 3:14-19)	**V** or **S (r)**
17. Ignatius of Antioch		**M** or **P**
bishop and martyr	Ph 3:17-4:1	III, 71
	Jn 12:24-26	III, 217
18. **Luke**	(I) 2 Tm 4:9-17a	—
evangelist	(G) Lk 10:1-9	V, 151
19. Isaac Jogues *priest and martyr* and companions *martyrs*		**M** or **P (m)**
Paul of the Cross *priest*	(1 Co 1:18-25)	**P** or **S (r)**
23. John Capistrano *priest*		**P (m)**
24. Anthony Claret *bishop*		**P (m)**
28. **Simon and Jude**	(I) Ep 2:19-22	VIII, 185
apostles	(G) Lk 6:12-16	VIII, 34

NOVEMBER

1. **ALL SAINTS**		IX, 79
2. **ALL SOULS**		IX, 136

3. Martin de Porres *religious*		**S (r)**
4. Charles Borromeo *bishop*		**P**
9. **Dedication of Saint John Lateran**		**C**
10. Leo the Great *pope and doctor*		**P (p)** or **D**
11. Martin of Tours *bishop*	Mt 25:31-40	**P** or **S (r)** III, 41
12. Josephat *bishop and martyr*		**M** or **P**
15. Albert the Great *bishop and doctor*		**P** or **D**
16. Margaret of Scotland		**S (m)**
Gertrude *virgin*	(Ep 3:14-19)	**V** or **S (r)**
17. Elizabeth of Hungary *religious*		**S (m or r)**
18. Dedication of the churches of Peter and Paul, *apostles*	(I) Ac 28:11-16, 30-31 (G) Mt 14:22-33	— V, 276
21. Presentation of Mary		**B.V.M.**
22. Cecilia *virgin and martyr*		**M** or **V**
23. Clement I *pope and martyr*		**M** or **P (p)**
Columban *abbot*		**P (m)** or **S (r)**
30. **Andrew** *apostle*	(I) Rm 10:9-18 (G) Mt 4:18-22	III, 19 II, 80

DECEMBER

3. Francis Xavier *priest*	(1 Co 9:16-19, 22-23 and Mk 16:15-20)	**P (m)**
4. John Damascene *priest and doctor*	(1 Tm 1:13-14; 2:1-3)	**P** or **D**
6. Nicholas *bishop*		**P**
7. Ambrose *bishop and doctor*		**P or D**
8. **IMMACULATE CONCEPTION**		IX, 88
11. Damasus I *pope*		**P (p)**

12. Jane Frances de Chantal *religious*		**S (r)**
13. Lucy *virgin and martyr*		**M** or **V**
14. John of the Cross *priest and doctor*	(1 Co 2:1-10a)	**P** or **D**
21. Peter Canisius *priest and doctor*		**P** or **D**
23. John of Kanty *priest*		**P**
26. **Stephen** *first martyr*		I, 222
27. **John** *apostle and evangelist*		I, 225
28. **Holy Innocents** *martyrs*		I, 228
29. Thomas Becket *bishop and martyr*		**M** or **P**
31. Sylvester I *pope*		**P (p)**

THIRD PART

BIOGRAPHY OF SAINTS OF THE UNIVERSAL CALENDAR*

* No biography is given of Mary (August 15), or of Peter and Paul (June 29). See the exegetical and doctrinal commentary concerning them in the text.

Achilles and Nereus (1st-2nd cent.) *May 12*

These two soldiers were certainly chamberlains of Flavia Domitilla, niece of the emperor Domitian. Being themselves Christian, they converted the girl, thus incurring exile and martyrdom. Their cult is very old in the Roman Church.

Agatha (3rd cent.) *February 5*

A Sicilian saint, the circumstances of whose martyrdom at Catania (in 251?) are unknown. Her cult spread in the West after the 6th century.

Agnes (4th cent.) *January 21*

A twelve year old Roman martyr (about 304). The spontaneity of her sacrifice made her cult very popular from the 4th century onward. Her laying down of life was a singular contrast with the massive defections that were ravaging the Roman community at this time.

Albert the Great (1200?-1280) *November 15*

Having studied at Padua before becoming a Dominican, Albert de Bollstaedt gained his mastership in theology at Paris where he became the professor of Thomas of Aquin. He was made a bishop but speedily resigned in order to return to his studies. He produced an admirable synthesis of natural science and theology, of philosophy and faith.

Aloysius of Gonzaga (1568-1591) *June 21*

At sixteen Aloysius renounced the throne of Mantua and entered the company of Jesus. When he died six years later, despite his impatient and impetuous temperament, grace had made him a saint. He overcame himself and gave himself entirely to charity. He died of a plague contracted during his ministrations.

Alphonsus Maria de Liguori (1696-1787) *August 1*

Alphonsus was a brilliant advocate at the Naples bar and sought the priesthood in order to devote himself to the evangelization of the poor. For this purpose he founded the Redemptorist order and placed his juridical knowledge in the service of moral theology and casuistry. He became a bishop and endured the greatest physical and psychological trials during his episcopate. He died expelled from his own order.

Ambrose (d. 397) *December 7*

Ambrose was governor of Milan, and while yet a catechumen was called to the episcopacy by the assembly of the faithful. He proved a remarkable pastor, sure in doctrine and profound. He played an important role in the composition of popular liturgical texts and in initiating catechumens to the Christian mysteries. He was also distinguished for the independence he showed in dealing with civil authorities, particularly the emperor Theodosius.

Andrew (1st cent.) *November 30*

The son of Jonas of Bethsaida (Mt 16:17) and younger brother of Peter, Andrew was the first disciple chosen by the Lord (Mt 4:18, above all Jn 1:40-42). His religious awakening was probably due to John the Baptist, in whose group he would have known the apostle John (Jn 1:35-40). In the apostolic group his interventions are not frequent, but they are significant. Peter was moved by his great enthusiasm to follow Christ (Jn 1:41). He it is also, who, faced with the hungry crowd, reminds Jesus of the miracle of manna and quails (Nb 21:21-23; cf. Jn 6:9), as if requesting him to repeat it.

With the Baptist doubtless he came into contact with essenism, and he evinces strong messianic hope. He asks the question to which Jesus responds by the eschatological discourse (Mk 13:3-37). He is also conscious of missionary need. With Philip he stands guarantor, according to prescribed Jewish requirements, for the good faith of the Gentiles who wanted to approach Christ (Jn 12:20-22).

Traditions which it is not possible to verify associate his apostolic work with Greece and Asia Minor. According to these he met his death on a "Saint Andrew's Cross."

Angela Merici (1474-1540) *January 27*

Born on the banks of the Lago di Garda in Italy, Angela realized that if Christianity were to successfully combat the surrounding paganism the family unit would have to be first restored. For this reason she founded the Ursuline Congregation to secure a Christian formation for future mothers. These would be made aware of the needs of their generation. The project was highly unusual at an epoch when there was no concept of Christian education for girls other than one behind the grille of the cloister.

Anne *July 26*

See **Joachim and Anne.**

Anschar (801-865) *February 3*

Anschar was born in Picardy and responded to the appeal of the recently converted King Harold to go as missionary to Denmark. He returned there a second time after having worked to spread the faith in north Germany. He occupied the sees successively of Hamburg and Bremen.

Anselm (1034-1109) *April 21*

Piedmontese by birth, Anselm became a monk in the Norman abbey of Bec-Hellouin and subsequently archbishop of Canterbury. His writings make him one of the precursors of scholastic theology. In his pastoral activities he was a defender of the liberty of the Church against the encroachments of civil power.

Anthony (251/252-357) *January 17*

"Sell what you have and follow me." This saying of Jesus was a sign for Anthony of vocation to the eremitic life. He retired to the desert of Upper Egypt, but quickly discovered the dangers of such solitude for those who are unprepared. Accordingly he initiated a formula of monastic rule where common life, prayer, the rule of a superior and fraternal charity proved more secure means of sanctification than eremetic practices.

Anthony of Padua (1195-1231) *June 13*

Anthony was born at Lisbon and entered the Franciscan order at the age of twenty-five. He contrived to go as missionary to Islam in the hope of obtaining martyrdom there. A storm forced him ashore in Italy on his return journey. Having preached in Lombardy and in the south of France, he succumbed during the course of a popular mission in Padua. Pius XII decreed for him the title "evangelic doctor" because of the profusion of scriptural quotations in his writings.

Anthony-Marie Claret (1807-1870) *October 24*

Having passed some years in the service of his native Church in Catalonia, Anthony founded the missionary congregation of the Immaculate Heart of Mary (Claretians). In 1850 he was made bishop of Santiago in Cuba by Pius IX, an area already torn by the crises that would reach their peak in the 20th century. Cuba is a rich country but has been so exploited by foreigners that natives cannot gain a decent livelihood. Anthony-Marie courageously sided with the oppressed, but he was obliged by his more powerful enemies to go into exile. He then devoted himself to preparations for the 1st Vatican Council.

Anthony-Marie Zaccaria (1502-1539) *July 5*

Born at Cremona (Italy), Anthony-Marie Zaccaria lived in the high noon of the Renaissance at a time when a triumphant humanism was rejecting Judaeo-Christian, biblical culture in favor of Graeco-Roman. He devoted his scriptural knowledge, particularly of Saint Paul, to the task of preaching the gospel and combatting pagan inroads. He founded for this purpose the order of Barnabites (so-called from the church of Saint-Barnabas in Rome, near which the new order was established).

Athanasius (4th century) *May 2*

When the persecutions ceased the Church of Alexandria experienced a period of intellectual activity that was not without vicissitudes. An Alexandrian priest called Arius, who was soon to be followed by a great number of bishops and leaders, denied the divinity of Christ, undermining Christian hope at its very roots. Athanasius, bishop of Alexandria, providentially became the principal defender of the faith inherited from the apostles. The Arian heresy nevertheless expanded in the East and West, with many ramifications, right up to the time of Charlemagne.

Augustine (354-430) *August 28*

After some experience of philosophy and a life of sin, Augustine was converted at the age of thirty-two. He was baptized by Ambrose of Milan. Returning to his native Africa he became bishop of Hippo. There he organized groups of clerics and virgins and displayed such pastoral and intellectual activity that he is rightly considered one of the pillars of Christian development in the West.

Augustine of Canterbury (d. 604) *May 27*

Augustine was a Roman monk, a disciple of Saint Gregory by whom he was sent as missionary to England. The pope's measure, though he did not know it, was a response to the wish of the Kentish king whose wife was already Christian. Augustine and the forty monks who accompanied him were well received and were soon able to proceed with the evangelization of Kent, laying the foundations of the Church in England.

Barnabas (1st century) *June 11*

Joseph was a member of the Jewish colony from Cyprus at Jerusalem, and was attached to the temple as a levite. He was converted in the early years of Christianity. Very soon his charity won him the name of Barnabas (son of encouragement). Throughout his whole life he was the conciliator *par excellence.* He introduced Paul to Judaeo-Christian circles (Ac 9:27; Ga 2:8-10), and was instrumental in the expansion of the Church of Antioch (Ac 11:22-30), which was the first instance of a church comprising more Greeks than Jews. He made the first missionary journey at the side of Paul, but the latter's over-strong personality forced him to continue his apostolate alone (Ac 15:36-40). Some believe that he may have been the compiler of the epistle to the Hebrews. His own priestly formation and his contact with Pauline thought would be a good preparation for the composition of this first treatise on the Christian priesthood.

Bartholomew (1st century) *August 24*

Except for the list of the apostles (Mt 10:3) Bartholomew is never mentioned in the New Testament. It is possibly he whom John calls Nathanael (Jn 1:45-51). Nothing is known of his apostolic activity.

Basil the Great (329-379) *January 2*

Basil had an innate feeling for organization. He was a monk at the age of twenty-five and by means of his various rules brought about a new monastic organization. At forty he became bishop of his native city of Caesarea (in Turkey). He strengthened the organization of the Church as against the civil power, founding a vast system of help for the poor, and in regulating the liturgy bequeathed to posterity one of the two great anaphoras of the Eastern Church. His numerous homilies and theological treatises have made him one of the four great Eastern doctors.

Bede the Venerable (672/3-735) *May 25*

Bede is the model medieval Benedictine. All his life was spent in the study of Scripture, chanting the office and compiling religious and secular treatises. He spent fifty years in the English abbey of Yarrow.

Benedict (480?-547) *July 11*

The rule proposed by Saint Benedict for Western monks is a happy blend of Eastern asceticism with Roman good sense and gospel prudence. He appeared at a propitious moment in the development of Western monasticism and the spread of the Church. He is regarded as the patriarch of those monks who converted all Europe in medieval times, thus assuring religious and cultural unit. For this reason he has been designated patron of Europe.

Bernard of Clairvaux (1090-1153) *August 20*

The second founder after a fashion of the Cistercian order, Bernard entered the abbey of Citeaux at the age of twenty-two, bringing with him thirty young men. He combined wisdom and contemplation with intense activity. He preached the second crusade, intervened as peace-maker in the quarrels dividing Christians and founded more than 150 monasteries. He compiled a great many commentaries on Scripture, which bear witness to his learning and his spiritual life, amply justifying his title as doctor of the Church.

Bernardine of Siena (1380-1444) *May 20*

An ardent missionary in Piedmont and Aquileia, this Franciscan, an indefatigable preacher, was the great 15th century propagator of devotion to the name of Jesus. His zeal brought him some opposition from theologians and Roman authorities.

Blaise (3rd-4th century) *February 3*

Bishop of Sebaste (Sivus in Turkey), Blaise was one of the last victims of Roman persecution (*circa* 316).

Bonaventure (1217/18-1274) *July 15*

The young John Fidanza, when miraculously cured by Saint Francis, changed his name to "Bonaventure" and entered the Franciscan order. He was for a considerable time professor of theology at Paris before becoming superior general of his order. He was the organizer of that order as the founder had left no precise constitution. He had to intervene in disputes between the followers of Saint Francis and in the conflicts, often exacerbated, between diocesan clergy and mendicant monks. He was made a cardinal and was able to bring about a project for Church reunion that was ratified by the Council of Lyons in 1274, but very soon afterwards shattered. His activity, and his considerable learning, were paralleled by a deep contemplative life that earned him the title of "Seraphic Doctor."

Boniface (672/5-754) *June 5*

An English Benedictine monk who was dispatched to the continent, Boniface is regarded as the greatest missionary of the high Middle Ages. His work in Germany was characterized by his monastic method and his great loyalty to Rome. He was martyred by the Frisians. The abbey of Fulda where his body rests, has continued to be the living center of German Catholicism.

Bridget (1302/3-1373) *July 23*

A wife and mother, belonging to the Swedish nobility, Bridget consecrated her widowhood to the Church. She was favored with supernatural visions. She journeyed to Rome where she labored for a reform of moral standards, and arranged for the return of the papacy from exile in Avignon.

Bruno (1030?-1101) *October 6*

Born at Cologne, Bruno of Hartenfaust was teaching theology at Rheims when he was forced to abandon his chair by the intrigues of an unworthy prelate. At the age of fifty he retired to the solitude of the Grand Chartreuse (near Grenoble) and subsequently to Calabria. He bequeathed a rule to the disciples who joined him in the eremetic life.

Cajetan (1480-1547) *August 7*

Cajetan was a prelate in the papal court, and felt himself drawn towards a more austere life. With his friend, the future Paul IV, he founded the first congregation of regulars, who wished, after the manner of the "monks" and the "mendicants," to respond to the needs of the time. Observance for them was confined to the monastic common life, but their spiritual life was very highly organized.

Callistus I (d. 222) *October 14*

Callistus was one of the great popes of the 3rd century. He organized Christian cemeteries, collecting the remains of the martyrs. He combatted the schism of Hippolytus and the rigorism of Tertullian by relaxing the regulations for admission to the catechumenate and for pardon of apostates. He died mysteriously during a scuffle between Jews and Christians. Documents of the 7th century regard him as a martyr.

Camillus of Lellis (1550-1614) *July 14*

A fairly tumultuous youth forced Camillus of Lellis to make a prolonged sojourn at the hospital for incurables in Rome. Discovering there the abject misery of the inmates, he decided to found a congregation of helpers for the sick who would replace the unworthy and incompetent nurses at the time.

Casimir (1458-1484) *March 4*

An hereditary prince of Poland and Lithuania, Casimir died of a wasting disease at the age of twenty-six. Though he lived in the luxury of the court he succeeded in maintaining a great love for the poor and in preserving his chastity. He is patron of Poland, and Lithuania where his relics are preserved. His feast was introduced to the universal calendar at a time when there was a desire to stress the solidarity of European states with the Holy See.

Catherine of Siena (1347?-1380) *April 29*

Catherine Benincasa entered the Third Order of Saint Dominic at the age of 19, and lived a life of austerity in her own house devoted to spiritual writing. During particularly troubled times she made many appeals for peace. She was instrumental in bringing the pope back to Rome from Avignon, and sowed the seeds of

Church reform. In the 14th century her task in concrete terms was one of making the Church emerge from the sociological structures of the middle ages, achieve greater unity and face effectively the new challenge that would be presented by the Renaissance and the Reformation.

Cecelia (2nd-3rd century) *November 22*

The cult of Saint Cecelia began in the 5th century with the celebrated legend concerning her, but her history is obscure. The discovery of her body in the 9th century was corroboration of her real existence.

Charles Borromeo (1538-1584) *November 4*

Charles was Secretary of State for his uncle Pius IV, and subsequently archbishop of Milan. His influence in making the decrees of the Council of Trent effective was decisive, through pastoral visitation, institution of seminaries, liturgical and catechetical directives, etc.

Charles Lwanga and his Companions (d. 1886) *June 3*

Scarcely seven years after the arrival of the first missionaries in Uganda, one hundred Christians, Catholics and Protestants, were brutally martyred. Twenty-two of them have been canonized and their leader, Charles Lwanga, proclaimed patron of African youth.

Clare (1194-1253) *August 11*

At the age of eighteen Clare became enthusiastic about the message of Saint Francis, and secured his agreement to her living the life of poverty proposed by him, with some companions, nearby. Thus was born the order of Poor Clares.

Clement 1 (1st century) *November 23*

Clement is the first successor of Peter whose existence can be confidently affirmed. Contrary to what was sometimes believed, he was not a companion of Paul. He is known chiefly for his letter to the Corinthians, the first indication of concern on the part of Rome for all the churches.

Cosmas and Damian (3rd-beginning 4th century)
September 26

These two Eastern saints, the date of whose martyrdom is unknown, were perhaps doctors. They were in any case thought to be such after their death, because of the great number of cures which took place at their tomb. September 26 is probably the anniversary of the dedication of the Roman Church raised in their honor.

Columban (543-615) *November 23*

This Irish monk played a decisive role in the re-Christianization of Western Europe during the Merovingian period. He founded numerous monasteries, in particular Luxeuil (France) and Bobbis (Italy). His extremely strict rule remained for a considerable time second only to that of Benedict in monastic life.

Cornelius and Cyprian (3rd century) *September 16*

On the 14th of September 258, when at Rome the relics of Pope Cornelius, who had died five years previously in exile, were being translated, Cyprian the bishop of Carthage underwent martyrdom in North Africa. By combining the Roman and African in the same celebration the liturgy reminds us of the close bonds between these churches that existed in the 3rd century.

Cyprian *September 16*

See **Cornelius and Cyprian.**

Cyril and Methodius (9th century) *February 14*

Dispatched to the Slavs by the Byzantine Church, particularly by the patriarch Photius who was then in the process of sundering from Rome, Cyril and Methodius as part of their mission translated the Bible into Slavonic and celebrated the liturgy in that language. They were anxious to lay the foundations of a genuine popular Christian culture. Their work however was beset by considerable difficulties, principally conflicts between Germans and Slavs. Byzantium not providing proper support in these troubles, the pair requested support from Rome. Only too glad to receive them, the pope ratified their mission and recognized their apostolic method, especially their liturgical procedure. Though slandered and frequently denounced, they remained always faithful to the essential rules of Christian apostolate: an adaptation of the message to the culture, a pursuit of unity rather than uniformity.

Cyril of Alexandria (d. 444) *June 27*

As patriarch of Alexandria, Cyril resolutely defended the dogma of Christ's unity of person. He presided at the Council of Ephesus which defined the divine motherhood of Mary and condemned Nestorius.

Cyril of Jerusalem (313?-387) *March 18*

Cyril is known above all for the catechetical instructions attributed to him. They reveal a pastor who is especially preoccupied with the formation of catechumens. His severe standards for the admission of candidates to baptism, and the depth of faith to which he leads them, are precious witness to the vitality of Christianity in the 4th century.

Damasus I (305?-384) *December 11*

Damasus, the bishop of Rome, was the first to effect a blend between the Church and Latin culture. He entrusted Saint Jerome with the task of translating the Bible into Latin, undertook the classification of Church archives, and laid the foundations of hagiography for the martyrs.

Damian *September 26*

See **Cosmas and Damian.**

Denis (3rd century) *October 9*

Denis, the first bishop of Paris, was one of a group of bishops and priests sent to Gaul by Pope Fabian. He, with his companions, died as a martyr in the environs of Paris. 9th Century legends confused him with Denis of Corinth (Acts 17:22-34).

Dominic (1170?-1221) *August 8*

Dominic Guzman, a Spanish canon, became aware in his thirty-fifth year of the missionary problem. He was commissioned by Pope Innocent III to combat the Albigensian heresy in the south of France. He took a lucid view of the actualities of the problem: the ignorance of the masses, clerical collusion with money and political power, the odious nature of some procedures of the inquisition. To deal with these he founded the order of friar preachers. They agreed to live the poor life of the people in order to train them in the true faith. They were a clergy independent of secular power and had sufficient confidence in the faith and liberty of the faithful to reject all procedures of conversion by force.

Elizabeth of Hungary (1207-1231) *November 17*

This Hungarian queen who died at the age of twenty-four was remembered as a woman altogether dedicated to succoring the poor, despite the numerous trials she had to undergo in her short life.

Elizabeth of Portugal (1270?-1336) *July 4*

Queen of Portugal from 1283 to 1325, Elizabeth was an unhappy bride and ill-requited mother. She sanctified her widowhood in the Third Order of Saint Francis.

Ephrem (306?-373) *June 9*

Ephrem was driven from Mossoul (Iraq) by the Persian invasion and became a deacon at Edessa (Syria). He was a perfect monk and a theologian fully alert to the heresies of his time.

Above all he was an accomplished poet, and composed many hymns that are prized in the Syriac liturgy.

Eusebius of Vercelli (283?-371) *August 2*

In 340 Eusebius was bishop of Vercelli (Italy). He endured such trials in his struggle with Arianism that he has been traditionally regarded as a martyr.

Fabian (3rd century) *January 20*

Fabian was bishop of Rome from 236 to 250 and showed remarkable administrative talent. He divided the city into seven deaconries for practical and charitable purposes. He died in the early stages of Decius' persecution.

Felicitas and Perpeuta (d. 202/3) *March 7*

The account of the martyrdom of these two Africans, one a slave and the other a noblewoman, is one of the most beautiful documents of early Christianity.

Fidelis of Sigmaringen (1578-1622) *April 24*

Born at Sigmaringen (Germany) Mark Roy became a celebrated advocate at Lolmar. He quit the bar in order to avoid using his talent for unworthy causes, and entered the Capuchins. As Father Fidelis he organized many preaching missions, placing his eloquence in the service of the gospel, particularly in Calvinist regions. During the course of one mission he was killed, at a stage when he had succeeded in opening dialogue with the reformers.

Frances of Rome (1384-1440) *March 9*

Of noble Roman stock, Frances was an exemplary wife and mother of a family. She was widowed at fifty-two and founded a congregation of Benedictive oblates.

Francis of Assisi (1181/82-1226) *October 4*

Francis took literally the counsel of imitating Christ. He is the originator of three great orders of men and women to whom he bequeathed a spirit rather than a rule. His style of holiness attracts all those for whom the spirit is more important than the letter, and love more important than justice.

Francis de Paul (1346-1507) *April 2*

Francis was a hermit in Calabria where he founded the order of minims. He attended the dying Louis XI and remained on in France to found a convent near Tours. Here, after a life spent in the love of God and the deepest humility, he died.

Frances de Sales (1567-1622) *January 24*

Francis was bishop of Geneva, but was prevented from living in that city by edict of the reformer magistrates. Nevertheless he succeeded in recovering part of his diocese for the Catholic faith. He devoted himself especially to forming the laity in the spiritual life, something that was previously regarded as a preserve of religious. With Jeanne deChantel he founded the Visitation order for the religious education of young girls. To him the Christian laity owe the first structures of a spirituality.

Francis Xavier (1506-1552) *December 3*

A fellow student of Ignatius of Loyola, Francis Xavier was one of the founders of the Jesuits, and the first Western missionary in India and Japan. He died at the frontiers of China. Renowned for his many miracles and conversions, his missionary style was nevertheless an indication of that which would be followed by Ricci and Nobili.

George *April 23*

As Eastern martyr of whom nothing is known but his name. The legend of the soldier who conquered the dragon was taken up by the Crusaders, who made George the patron of their military and chivalric projects.

Gertrude (1256-1302) *November 16*

A Benedictine nun of Helfta in Saxony, Gertrude found in the liturgy and meditation on the Scriptures the basis for an intense contemplative life. Her writings contributed especially to the diffusion of cult of the Sacred Heart.

Gregory the Great (540?-604) *September 3*

Gregory was civil prefect of Rome and retired to monastic life for contemplation of the divine mysteries through meditation on Scripture. He was subsequently sent as papal representative to Constantinople. Becoming bishop of Rome, he was careful to organize the liturgy, collating all the sources which predated his reign, and composing prayers that are often strongly marked by his desire for heaven and his disillusionment with earthly things. He sent monks to Gaul and England. All medieval piety was influenced strongly by his spiritual writings, which made him one of the four great doctors of the Western Church.

Gregory VII (1020/25-1085) *May 25*

A Benedictine monk of Cluny, Hildebrand devoted all his life to Church reform. A counselor first to Alexander II, he in turn became pope in 1075, taking the name Gregory. By bringing the Church out of its medieval confusion between the spiritual and the temporal, by liberating it from political constraint, he was preparing the Church of modern times. But for the ideal of purity which he set for it he was to pay with exile.

Gregory of Nazianzen (330-390) *January 2*

Born near Nazianzen (Menizi in Turkey) Gregory completed his studies in Athens. He developed a fast friendship with Basil, whose monastic ideal he shared. And like Basil he became a bishop, at Nazianzen first, then at Constantinople. This last see he occupied during a troubled period, and his sensitive nature could not endure the difficulties he encountered. He resigned to devote himself to the composition of theological works. These are among the most profound that the Eastern Church has given us.

Hedwig (d. 1243) *October 16*

Hedwig was duchess of Silena and mother of six children. Her sanctity was achieved as mistress of a household and during a widowhood of great trial. She withdrew to the Cistercian monastery of Trebnitz.

Henry (973-1024) *July 13*

Emperor of the West, Henry was an outstanding servant of the Church. He organized dioceses and monasteries and was an example of all the virtues.

Hilary (315?-367) *January 13*

Hilary was bishop of Portiers and an ardent defender of the doctrines of the Trinity and Christ's divinity. His zeal in combatting Arianism made him an exile to the East. A sojourn there of four years he used to deepen his knowledge of Eastern theology, and he afterwards communicated this knowledge to the West.

Hippolytus (d. 235) *August 13*

Hippolytus was a Roman priest and strenuously opposed Pope Callistus. Callistus, who was perhaps of African origin, had introduced new usages at Rome that were more suited to people's attitude and the times. Hippolytus, who was frantically attached to the ancient ways, reacted very vigorously. To this we owe an important document, *Apostolic Tradition,* that was compiled by Hippolytus himself. His attitude brought him near the border of schism, but the exile of the two protagonists in the dispute brought about reconciliation in a common martyrdom.

Ignatius of Antioch (d. 118) *October 17*

Bishop of Antioch in Syria, Ignatius was condemned to the beasts at Rome. He wrote letters of thanks to all the churches who had received him on his journey. They reveal his eucharistic concept of martyrdom, as a culmination of the liturgical sacrifice of love and obedience. He wants to become the "white bread of Christ" by giving up his life.

Ignatius of Loyola (1391-1556) *July 31*

A daring and adventurous soldier, it was during a long convalescence from a severe wound that Ignatius discovered Christ and the needs of the Church. In founding the Jesuits he provided the pope with a necessary tool for combatting heretical ideas, reforming the Church and expanding it to faraway places. In order that his group might be more efficacious, Ignatius freed them from choral recitation of the office, but imposed otherwise a very severe spiritual discipline, the basic charter being the "Spiritual Exercises." The group as a result became extremely open to the culture of their time.

Irenaeus (d. 202?) *June 28*

Irenaeus was of Asiatic origin but settled quite early at Lyons in Gaul. He succeeded Pothinus as bishop of that city, and laid the foundations of theology in the West by means of his doctrinal writings against syncretists and gnostics.

Isaac Jogues (17th century) *October 19*

See **John de Brebeuf, Isaac Jogues and companions.**

Isidore (560?-636) *April 4*

In Isidore, the bishop of Seville, the Spanish Church venerates one of its greatest bishops. He was responsible for the organization of the "Mozarbic" liturgy which combined Roman austerity with the poetic genius of his own people and the religious sentiment of the East. He was in addition a great encyclopedist, and his numerous "dictionaries" became the basic corpus of medieval knowledge.

James the Greater (1st century) *July 25*

Called by Jesus at the same time as his brother John (Mt 4:21; Lk 5:10) James was a friend of the Lord. He was privileged to assist at several miracles, notably the transfiguration (Mt 17) and the agony in the garden (Mk 14:33), thus filling the role of witness according to Jewish law. He showed considerable zeal for the Kingdom (Mk 3:17; Lk 9:54; cf. 2 K 1:10-12), but sometimes sought his own interest (Mt 20:20-23). Jesus' prophecy that he would drink the chalice with him was fulfilled to the letter. He was the first apostle to lay down his life in martyrdom, during the actual feast of the Pasch, like his Lord (Ac 12:1).

James the Less (1st century) *May 3*

James, called the Less to distinguish him from the preceding James, is known as the son of Alphaeus (Mt 10:3; Mk 3:18; Ac 1:13). That he was the brother of the Lord who ruled the Jerusalem community (Ac 12:17; 15-13; Ga 1:19) seems doubtful.

Jane Frances de Chantal (1572-1641) *December 12*

Widowed at twenty-eight Jeanne Frances met Francis de Sales, who directed her to the most intense religious life. Her spiritual way, characterized by Salesian discretion and finesse, led to the foundation of the Visitation order.

Januarius *September 19*

Two bishops of Benevento bore this name. It is unclear which is in question; the first who died as martyr during the persecution of Diocletian, or the second, who was exiled by the Arians in 350.

Jerome (347?-420) *September 30*

Born near the frontiers of modern Yugoslavia and Hungary, Jerome studied at Rome, where he was baptized. During a journey to Treves (Germany) he became acquainted with monasticism and retired to Syria to live the eremetic life. He was ordained a priest at Antioch and returned to Rome as secretary of Pope Damasus. With Damasus he accomplished the project of translating the whole Bible into Latin, in order to replace faulty previous renderings. To complete this work, destined to become the Vulgate, he retired to Jerusalem, and diversified the work by the spiritual direction of some nuns and Roman ladies.

Jerome Emiliani (1486-1537) *February 8*

Like Saints Camillus and Vincent, Jerome is a witness to Christian charity. He devoted himself especially to orphans, abandoned girls and children. He founded for this purpose the Congregation of "Somascans," so-called from the name of the small village where it began.

Joachim and Anna (1st century) *July 26*

These were the parents of the Virgin Mary. They are given the names Joachim and Anna by the proto-gospel of James (3rd cent.). The cult of the pair is due to Eastern liturgy. It was customary in the East to celebrate thus with parents the birth of a child.

John (1st century) *December 27*

John was son of Zebedee, a wealthy fisherman of Bethsaida (Mk 1:20; Mt 4:18-22; Jn 1:44), and Salome, one of the women who served Jesus and the apostles (Lk 8:3; 23:55; 24:10). Doubtless, like his brother James, he had been formed in the Zealot sect, and this is corroborated by the liveliness of his exchange (Mk 3:17; 20:20-23; Lk 9:53-56). He became a disciple of John the Baptist and was sent to Jesus by the Baptist. He immediately became one of the most active in Jesus' group, and one of those to whom Jesus entrusted the greatest number of tasks and secrets (Mt 17:1-8; Mk 13:3; Lk 22:8; Jn 13:23; Mt 26:37; Jn 19:26; 20:3). He took part in the Council of Jerusalem (Ga 2:9), and after a long career as apostle was exiled by the emperor Domitian (Rev 1) to the island of Patmos.

His gospel is centered on the manifestation of God in the world in the person of Jesus. To this he gives the name "witness" or "sending." The manifestation consists above all in a series of "signs" of God's "glory," the most important taking place at the "hour" of Jesus' glorification in the paschal mystery. These signs are perpetuated in the life of the Church and in the sacraments of the Lord's presence.

John 1 (d. 526) *May 18*

John was elected pope in 523. He was a victim of persecution under Arian king Theodoric, and died of hunger in a Ravenna prison.

John the Baptist (1st century) *June 24*

John was son of Zechariah who was mute, and Elizabeth who was sterile. His birth heralded the advent of the messianic age when the sterile was destined to be fruitful, the dumb to speak in prophecy. He is given the name "Baptist" by the gospel because he proclaimed a new rite of ablution (Mt 3:13-17). Here the recipient not only plunged himself in the water as in Jewish rites, but also received the water from the hands of the minister, to show that all holiness comes from God. He also left the reputation of great asceticism. Possibly he was initiated to this among the Jewish desert communities.

Tradition regarded him chiefly as a prophet however, a role that he fulfills under two heads. He was such in the Old Testament sense, was indeed the greatest of the prophets of Israel, because he was able to point out with his finger the very object of his oracles (Mt 11:7-15; Jn 1:19-28). More important, he was essentially a carrier of the Word of God, and the witness of the presence of this creative Word in the new world.

John Baptist de la Salle (1651-1714) *April 7*

John was born at Reims, and in founding the brothers of the Christian schools brought about a considerable revolution in the training of youth. He was the first to replace Latin with the vernacular as the language of instruction, and thus laid the foundations of general popular education. He developed solid pedagogic principles. The congregation he founded was the first lay one, uncontrolled by priests. His spirituality and his constitutions, inspired by the French school of the 17th century, for long remained the model for other congregations of brothers.

John Bosco (1815-1888) *January 31*

After particularly arduous study John was ordained a priest, but remained mindful of his humble origins. He devoted his priestly life to the poor, the destitute and abandoned children. In helping them spiritually and materially, he displayed an extraordinary trust in Providence and was able to accomplish the most difficult enterprises. He founded at Turin the congregation of Salesians and the institute of Marie Auxiliatrice.

John Capistrano (1386-1456) *October 23*

John was an Italian Franciscan who traveled all the East by order of the popes of the time to form a coalition of Christian princes against the Turks. He himself commanded the forces of the West before Belgrade where he won a decisive victory some months before his death.

John Chrysostom (350?-407) *September 13*

Born at Antioch, John retired to solitude for some years before receiving the priesthood and becoming bishop of Constantinople. His remarkable eloquence he devoted to stigmatizing the vices and disorders of the imperial court. He died when on the way to exile. With good reason he is regarded as one of the four great doctors of the Eastern Church.

John of the Cross (1542-1591) *December 14*

Entering Carmel in 1563 at a time when the rule was considerably relaxed. John undertook the task of restoring it to primitive observance. His efforts led to his expulsion from the convent and imprisonment. These trials enabled him to discover the mystery of the cross and enter a path of the highest contemplation.

John Damascene (670?-750) *December 4*

Of Christian Arabian background, John Damascene held an important post for a considerable time at the caliph's court. In this capacity he reacted violently to a decision of the Byzantine emperor suppressing statues and images in churches. Intrigues by the emperor culminated in his expulsion from the caliph's court. He then retired to the monastery of Saint Sabas where he devoted himself to theological studies. In these he distills the essential doctrine of the Greek fathers who preceded him, and whose flourishing line he brings to a close.

John de Brebeuf, Isaac Jogues and companions (17th century) *October 19*

Less than a century after the discovery of Canada, the French came to found New France. They were followed by the Jesuit missionaries. A bloody struggle soon ensued between the French and the Iroquois, who were armed by the English and Dutch. In it were massacred John de Brebeuf, Isaac Jogues and their companions.

John Eudes (1601-1680) *August 19*

John Eudes' piety was of the French school, thoroughly influenced by devotion to the hearts of Jesus and Mary. His missionary apostolate was directed towards the re-Christianization of rural areas. Recent sociological study has shown that the areas touched by this missionary effort of the 17th century are still Christian though other places are thoroughly de-Christianized. It is a remarkable tribute to the work of John Eudes and his companions.

John Fisher (1469?-1535) *June 22*

Born in Yorkshire, John studied and was subsequently a professor at Cambridge. In 1504 he became bishop of Rochester. He did not hesitate to oppose Henry VIII in the matter of divorce, and was consequently arrested and executed with his friend Thomas More.

John of God (1495-1550) *March 8*

A great witness to Christian charity, without money or companions, John organized a hospital at Granada for the poor. His trust in divine Providence and the charity of his fellow Christians enabled him to succeed, and he laid the foundations of the Hospitallers of Saint John of God.

John of Kanty (1390-1473) *December 23*

John was a professor at the University of Krakow, and became celebrated for his numerous pilgrimages to Rome and Jerusalem. Because of his extraordinary charity to the poor he holds an honored place in the Polish "century of saints."

John Leonardi (1541-1609) *October 9*

John Leonardi's life is marked by three important projects: the foundation of the company of clerics of the mother of God dedicated to popular education and the ministry of the sacraments, the setting up of the important Propaganda college in Rome, and the service of plague victims. He himself fell victim to his concern for the sick.

John Marie Vianney (1786-1859) *August 4*

The youth of John Marie coincided with the beginnings of the French revolution and his priesthood with the political upheavals of the early 19th century, which were the birth pangs of the modern world. Above all he wanted to be a true pastor. His course in theology caused him great difficulty, and his sermons were no more than fairly arbitrary extracts from the collections of his time. His catechetics were poor by modern standards. Nevertheless his pastoral method was extraordinarily effective because it was based on the essential: a group of people gathered for salvation, accomplished in the Christian assembly by means of sacraments and the Word.

Josaphat (1580-1623) *November 12*

The history of most European countries is marked by the struggle between East and West, and it was this that led to the martyrdom of Josaphat. He was coadjutor bishop of Polotsk, and induced his Ruthenian compatriots to submit to Rome. This was partly for religious reasons (the Moscow patriarchate had just been set up) and partly for political. More ardent than prudent in his pursuit of his ideal, he paid with his life for his devotion to the Holy See.

Joseph (1st century) *March 19*

A humble tradesman at Nazareth, it was the mission of Joseph to provide davidic ancestry for Jesus, a requirement according to the Scriptures of Messiahship. The gospel of Matthew likes to attribute "dreams" to him after the manner of the patriarchs (Mt 1:20-24; 2:13-19). This is a way of recognizing his decisive role in salvation history. He is the last of the patriarchs. When he flees to Egypt with his family, it is to undertake the journey of the patriarch Joseph, so that the new Exodus may be accomplished in him, and in Jesus (Mt 2:13-23; Ho 11-1; Gn 37; 50:22-26).

Joseph Calasanz (1556/57-1648) *August 25*

A Spaniard by birth, Joseph settled at Rome, and some years before John Baptist de la Salle, founded the first popular schools. He formed a congregation of clerics to control them. He was however rejected by his own congregation and pursued by Roman authority to the point where the schools were closed. He imposed silence on himself and chose resignation as a path to holiness.

Jude (1st century) *October 28*

See **Simon and Jude.**

Justin (100?-165) *June 1*

Justin was a Palastinian philosopher and placed his knowledge at the service of the Church. At a time when the formation of catechumens was not yet organized systematically, he made his school of "Christian philosophy" a sort of preparatory catechesis for baptism. In the same way he used his knowledge of pagan thought for the composition of some apologies that presented Christianity as a fulfillment of human wisdom.

Lawrence (d. 258) *August 10*

Lawrence was arrested at the same time as Pope Sixtus. He was an archdeacon, and was spared in the hope that some information concerning the community could be wrested from him. Some days later he was burned alive, when he affirmed that he had no other riches but the poor cared for by the Church.

Lawrence of Brindisi (1559-1619) *July 21*

A man of deep culture, this Capuchin from Verona placed his scriptural knowledge at the service of the Church after the Council of Trent. He engaged in military crusades against the Turks, and proved useful in papal diplomacy. Throughout he remained a true son of Saint Francis, kind to everybody, simple and humble.

Leo the great (d. 461) *November 10*

Leo was bishop of Rome from 440 onwards, at a time when Rome was besieged and pillaged by barbarians. He was one of the great popes. In 451 he convened the Council of Chalcedon, which defined the doctrine of two natures and one person in Christ. The doctrine influenced him profoundly in the compilation of the Roman liturgy for Christmas.

Louis (1219-1270) *August 25*

Louis IX of France drew inspiration for his goals of unity and reconcilation from his Catholic faith. He was charitable towards the poor and the sick, and was devoted to the holy places that he organized a crusade. This culminated in defeat for his armies and his own death.

Lucy (beginning of 4th century) *December 13*

A virgin and martyr under Diocletian. In Sicily her popularity was great. On December 13 what is celebrated is probably the anniversary of a translation of her relics or the dedication of a church in her honor.

Luke (1st century) *October 18*

Luke was born at Antioch and was exercising his profession as doctor when he was converted (Col 4:14). He placed himself in the service of Saint Paul (Phm 24; 2 Tm 4:11; Ac 16:10-17; 20: 5-21:28), and doubtless assisted at his last moments (2 Tm 4:11). His Gentile background and his association with Paul were an ideal preparation for the composition of the gospel of the Gentiles. The basic ideas are salvation for all nations (3:6; 7:1-9; 13:28-30), and a share in the Kingdom for all the classes that had been excluded from worship by Jewish law: the poor, weak sinners, women and Gentiles (5:29-32; 7:26-8:3; 10:21-22).

Luke was particularly attached to Jerusalem, the city from which salvation spread to the world. The events of Jesus' life he groups around his ascents to Sion and he describes the life of the primitive Jerusalem community in glowing terms (Ac 2:42-47; 4:32-35; 5:12-16).

Marcellinus and Peter (d. 304) *June 2*

These were Roman martyrs under Diocletian. They were buried in the catacombs of Saint Tiburtius on the Via Labicana.

Margaret of Scotland (1045-1093) *November 16*

Margaret became queen of Scotland after much tribulation. She lived a model family life, exercising considerable influence over her husband and children, and always welcoming the poor.

Margaret Mary Alacoque (1647-1690) *October 16*

This religious was favored with revelations that are the basis of modern devotion to the Sacred Heart. At a time when Jansenist rigorism was congealing spirits, this humble nun bore witness to the true religion of the gospel, a religion of faith in the incarnation, of love and of sacramental life.

Maria Goretti (1890-1902) *July 6*

This twelve year old Italian girl, of humble birth, resisted several assaults on her virtue by a neighbor, who finally carried out his threats to kill her. At the moment of death she pardoned her murderer.

Mark (1st century) *April 25*

John Mark (Ac 12:12, 24; 15:37) belonged to a hellenizing family at Jerusalem, who placed their house at the disposal of the early Christians (Ac 12:12-16). It is believed that the house may have been used already by Jesus and the disciples and that the Last Supper may have taken place there. Mark went with Paul on his first journey (Ac 12:25; 13:5), but does not seem to have shared his leader's enthusiasm. He returned to Jerusalem alone (Ac 13:13), and was the occasion of a sharp exchange between Paul and Barnabas when the second journey was being organized (Ac 15:39-41). He then followed Peter to Rome and served him during his imprisonment (Col 4:10), and when Paul in turn became a prisoner he was at his disposition too (2 Tm 4:11).

His gospel is marked by a very special characteristic: the sad contrast between Jesus, who is endowed with the divine prerogatives of healing (1:31), pardon (2:10) and power over demons (1:24-27; 3:11, 23; 4:41; 5:7), and men who mock him (5:40; 6:2; 15:29-32) and wish to destroy him (2:1; 3:6; 14:1). The "scandal" of this contrast he explains by the paschal mystery itself (Mk 16), but he sees it also as the fulfillment of some law of the divine plan itself (8:31; 9:31; 10:33), something that is found in every Christian life (8:34; 9:35; 10:24-39; 13:9-13).

Martha (1st century) *July 29*

Martha was the sister of Mary and Lazarus and is noted as Christ's chosen hostess (Jn 11; 12:1-11; Lk 10:38-42). He is present also in our eucharistic assemblies, and expects the same eager cooperation with his plans.

Martin 1 (d. 655) *April 13*

Martin was bishop of Rome for six years. He defended the faith against the "monothelites" who refused to allow Jesus a free human will. This would undermine his capacity to merit, and would endanger the doctrine of redemption and our cooperation. The Byzantine emperor, who took part in the controversy for political reasons, exiled Martin to the Crimea.

Martin de Porres (1579-1639) *November 3*

The natural son of a nobleman in Lima and a servant girl, Martin was reared by his mother and then took orders. He is noted for his great kindness to the sick and the poor.

Martin of Tours (316/17-397) *November 11*

Martin is one of the great figures of the Gaulish Church. He was born in Pannonia (Hungary), and served for several years in the Roman army before coming to Gaul and attending the school of Saint Hilary. On Hilary's advice he founded the abbey of Ligugé. Ten years later he became bishop of Tours by popular wish. Again he founded a monastery at Marmoutier which became both a spiritual and a missionary center. At a time when the center of gravity was shifting from the cities to the country, he gave special attention to rural evangelization. His name is associated with the foundation of parishes in Gaul.

Mary Magdalene (1st century) *July 22*

Mary was a native of Magdala in Galilee. She was cured by Jesus (Lk 8:2), and devoted herself to his service. She helped at his burial and was the first to recognize the Risen Lord. The evidence for identifying her with the sister of Martha is slight, as is that for identifying her with the sinful woman (Lk 7:36-50).

Mary Magdalene de Pazzi (1566-1607) *May 25*

Mary entered Carmel at the age of fifteen, and lived a life of prayer and the most extraordinary mortification.

Matthias (1st century) *May 14*

A native of Bethlehem, Matthias was one of those who followed Jesus during his public ministry. When it became necessary to fill the place of Judas the disciples put him forward with Barnabas the Just. The lot fell on Matthias, and he was added to the Eleven (Ac 1:16-26). These are the only details we have concerning the life of this apostle.

Matthew (1st century) *September 21*

A collector of taxes and publican at Capharnaum, Matthew was a cultivated man. Due to his hellenistic formation he had probably hellenized his Jewish name, Levi (Mk 2:14; Lk 5:27). His role in the transmission of the gospel was capital. After the resurrection, some episodes from Jesus' life had been collected and narratives were joined together by key words, which would resemble the readings that the first Christians were still hearing in the synagogues. Matthew made a synthesis of these, a sort of *aide-memoire* for preachers. He did so in Aramaic, concentrating because of the apologetic needs of the time on the proofs of Jesus' Messiahship, and the arguments to justify Christian attitudes to legal observance. We are altogether ignorant of the other details of Matthew's career as apostle and his death.

Methodius *February 14*

See **Cyril and Methodius.**

Monica (332?-387) *August 27*

We know the life of Saint Augustine's mother through his "confessions." An ardent Christian, she succeeded in converting her husband through gentleness, and her son through tears.

Nereus *May 12*

See **Achilleus and Nereus.**

Nicholas (4th century) *December 6*

Nicholas was bishop of Myra and we do not have any genuinely historical data concerning him. From the 6th century onwards his cult was popular at Constantinople, and it reached the West after his relics were translated to Bari in 1087.

Norbert (1082?-1134) *June 6*

Norbert was one of the great architects of the reform of Gregory VII, which was aimed at securing autonomy for the Church from political powers. He began with himself, severing in his own life all political associations. This he imposed on his clerics too, proposing for them a way of life that would withdraw them from the tentacles of feudalism, when he founded the Premonstratensian order. Subsequently, as bishop of Magdeburg in Germany, he imposed the Gregorian reform in his diocese, elevating the standard of clerical behavior, and liberating the Church from dependence on the local lords.

Pancras (d. 304) *May 12*

A young martyr during the persecution of Diocletian. He was beheaded for refusing to sacrifice to idols. A basilica was erected over his tomb about 500.

Patrick (385?-461) *March 17*

The first apostle of Ireland, Patrick was born in the environs of Boulogne-sur-Mer. He was a monk at Saint Martin of Tours and left his monastery to evangelize Ireland, which he knew from a sojourn there when captured by pirates. His mission was immediately crowned with success. Succeeding centuries were to confirm the quality of the seed he sowed in this "island of saints."

Paul of the Cross (1694-1775) *October 19*

Paul was born near Genoa in Italy in the same year as Voltaire. Assisted by his brother John he was to devote his whole life to bearing witness to the folly of the cross in an age of scepticism. He founded the order of Passionists, dedicated to preaching the mystery of the cross in a materialistic and scientific world.

Paulinus of Nola (353?-431) *June 22*

Paulinus belonged to a family of Roman *coloni* which owned considerable property near Bordeaux. He abandoned the world to live the eremetic life and retired to his property at Nola (south Italy), where he became bishop. During the Gothic invasions he showed great charity towards the harassed faithful, selling all his goods to assist them.

Paul Miki and his companions (d. 1597) *February 6*

Thirty years after its beginnings under Francis Xavier, the mission in Japan encountered grave difficulties. The authorities arrested six Franciscans, three Jesuits, of whom the most celebrated was Paul Miki, and seventeen laymen. After mistreatment of every kind these men were condemned to death, and finally crucified at the seashore near Nagasaki.

Perpetua *March 7*

See **Felicity and Perpetua.**

Peter Canisius (1521-1597) *December 21*

Peter was born at Nijmegen in the lowlands and entered the company of Jesus. He gave himself totally to the work of Catholic reform, by preaching, by manuals of doctrine and by the foundation of several Jesuit colleges in Germany. Frequently he acted as intermediary between the pope and German princes, and the strength of Catholicism in Germany and Austria is in large measure due to his decisive action then. His celebrated catechism, put together for an apologetic purpose, was the beginning of modern Christian education.

Peter Chanel (1803-1841) *April 28*

Born near Belley, Peter Chanel had nine months ministry in France before departing as missionary to Oceania. There at

Futuna, the initial benevolence of the king swiftly changed to opposition. The conversion of his son made him decide to suppress this missionary, and Peter Chanel became the first martyr of the new Marist congregation.

Peter Chrysologus (380?-450) *July 30*

Bishop of Ravenna, Peter was one of the great pastors of his age. His popular preaching and his doctrine earned him the title of doctor of the Church.

Peter Damian (1007-1072) *February 21*

Peter was a Camaldolese hermit and was made cardinal-bishop of Ostia by Pope Stephen IX. He was able to work effectively at liberating the Church from temporal involvement, combatting the intellectual and moral decadence of the clergy, and laying the basis of the reform that Gregory VII was soon to undertake. In order to reform the Church however, Peter had to prepare himself by a life of holiness and austerity.

Philip (1st century) *May 3*

Philip was one of the first disciples (Jn 1:43). Though a native of Bethsaida, like the other disciples who followed Jesus at the same time, he must have belonged to a somewhat hellenized community, if we are to judge from his name and his association with Gentiles (Jn 12:20-30). The three interventions by him that we know from the gospels (Jn 1:45; 6:5-7; 14:8) are concerned with the Old Testament, and show his concern that the prophecies be realized in the person of Christ. He helps us see the multiplication of loaves in the light of Exodus (Nb 11:21-23). His request "show us the Father" recalls that of Moses "show us your glory" (Ex 33:18). It is uncertain whether we should accept the tradition that places his mission and martyrdom in Turkey.

Philip Neri (1515-1595) *May 26*

Philip landed at Rome at the age of twenty-one and lived the saintly life there according to a cloistral pattern, occasionally somewhat eccentric, but always turned towards God. After being ordained a priest he gathered round him in a varified atmosphere a group of young men who aspired to a higher religious life. This was the Oratory group, established on a basis similar to congregations of secular clergy.

Pius V (1504-1572) *April 30*

Pius, who had entered the Dominicans at the age of fourteen, became pope at the age of sixty-two. During the six years of his pontificate he made the decisions of the Council of Trent operative. In the domain of liturgy he put out a new missal and breviary, in catechetics the "catechism of the Council of Trent"; and in theology he introduced the Summa of Saint Thomas to the universities.

Pius X (1835-1914) *August 21*

A humble peasant from Riese (Italy) Joseph Sarto passed through all the degrees of the clerical hierarchy, becoming pope finally under the name Pius X. He is one of the few popes of modern times who passed from the most humble pastoral life to the papacy. This pastoral experience profoundly influenced his reign, especially where liturgy was concerned. He opened the way to the liturgical reforms we know today.

Polycarp (70?-155/56) *February 23*

Bishop of Smyrna (Turkey) Polycarp was the last disciple of Saint John. Condemned to the executioner, he made a sacrifice of his martyrdom, rendering thanks to God that he shared the chalice of the Lord.

Pontianus (d. 235) *August 13*

A bishop of Rome who was exiled by the emperor Alexander Severus.

Raymond of Penyafort (1175/80-1275) *January 7*

A Barcelona noble, Raymond became a priest after considerable theology study and entered the Dominican Order at the age of forty-seven. He became a celebrated confessor and a learned canonist, putting together one of the first codifications of ecclesiastical law. His primary title to fame however is his project for the conversion of Islam. He organized a religious order for the ransom of Christian prisoners of the Moslems, the members to be trained in knowledge of Arabic and the Koran.

Robert Bellarmine (1542-1621) *September 17*

Robert, a Florentine by birth, entered the Jesuit order at the age of eighteen and became step by step a professor at Louvain, a counselor of popes, provincial of the Jesuits and cardinal archbishop of Capua. He was chiefly distinguished for his doctrinal controversies with Lutherans and Calvinists, and for the preparation of a "little catechism," which reflects the polemic of the 17th century, but served as a tool of Christian education for a considerable time. His catechetical work and his influence in the formation of generations of Christians have earned him the title of doctor of the Church.

Romuald (952?-1027) *June 19*

Romuald was a descendant of the dukes of Ravenna. He adapted the rule of Saint Benedict to the eremetic life and founded the Camaldolese order, which still today comprises a few hundred hermits.

Rose of Lima (1586-1617) *August 23*

From her adolescent years onwards Isabelle d'Oliva, called Rose because of her fresh complexion, was involved with the Third Order of Dominicans. She dedicated her life to the needs of the poor and to the normal family duties of a young girl. She died at Lima at the age of thirty-one. She was the first saint from the American continent to be canonized, a century after its discovery by Christopher Columbus.

Scholastica (480?-457?) *February 10*

Scholastica was a sister of Saint Benedict and followed her brother into the monastic life. She seems to have gathered a group of nuns around her.

Sebastian (4th century) *January 20*

Sebastian was a soldier from Milan. When sent on duty to Rome he refused to carry out certain cruel tasks because of his faith. For his conscientious objection he paid with his life.

Seven Servites (13th century) *February 17*

These were seven Florentine merchants who laid aside their trade to seek holiness by imitation of the Virgin. This was the beginning of the Servite order.

Simon and Jude (1st century) *October 28*

History is silent concerning these two apostles. In the New Testament Simon is given the name Zealot (Mt 10:4; Ac 1:13), because of his attachment probably to the Jewish theocratic and messianic ideal, and his opposition to the Romans. There is mention of a Simon and Jude among the "brethren of the Lord" (Mt 13:55), but there is no basis for identifying them with the apostles.

Sixtus II (d. 258) *August 7*

Pope Sixtus was discovered while celebrating the Eucharist by the troops of the emperor Valerian. He and his clergy were immediately executed, thus bringing the liturgy to its consummation.

Stanislaus (1030-1079) *April 11*

As archbishop of Krakow, Stanislaus did not hesitate to excommunicate the Polish king, whose conduct was causing scandal. The king avenged himself by personally executing him.

Stephen (1st century) *December 26*

From Acts 6:1-6 we know the circumstances of Stephen's election among the "Seven." There was some tension between Christians of Jewish origin and those of Gentile, and each group ran the risk of isolation. The apostles were conscious of their own basic responsibilities (Rm 15:20; 1 Co 3:10; 12:28; Rev 21:14) and passed on to others certain tasks of organization and preaching. The Greek background of the "Seven" neutralized to some extent the authority of the Jewish "elders."

Stephen however did not limit his activity to charitable services only (Ac 6:1), but engaged in preaching and evangelization. Accordingly we have from him a discourse which is the first attempt at a Christian rereading of Old Testament texts in the context of the Lord's coming (Ac 7). It was to be the charter of the first missionaries.

The first "deacon," the first apologist, Stephen is also the first martyr in the Church. His combative style proved intolerable to those whom his attack pursued even to their synagogues. He paid with his life for alleged blasphemies.

Stephen of Hungary (969?-1038) *August 16*

The evangelization of Hungary, an undertaking principally of the Byzantine Church, was in the 11th century seriously compromised because the Eastern Church had lost its ancient prestige. From a political point of view Stephen became aware of the danger, and opted for the West, adopting its manners and culture. He had himself consecrated king by the pope in 1001, favored the organization of dioceses after the Roman pattern and entrusted Czech and Bavarian Benedictines with responsibility for the Church in his territory.

Sylvester 1 (d. 335) *December 31*

Just after the peace of Constantine, Pope Sylvester concerned himself with organizing the Church at Rome and building the first great basilicas where the people could assemble on great feasts. He made good use of the emperor's services in convoking the first ecumenical council at Nicaea. In this fashion he laid the doctrinal and disciplinary framework for the new status of the Church.

Teresa of Avila (1515-1582) *October 15*

When Teresa entered the Carmel of Avila, it resembled many other congregations in its mitigated observance. Having subjected herself to especial rigors she undertook, with the assistance of John of the Cross, the reform of her order. Despite the constant activity required by the foundation of new convents, and the many difficulties she had to encounter, she reached the summit of mystical contemplation.

Therese of the Child Jesus (1873-1897) *October 1*

Because of her persistence Therese Martin gained permission to enter Carmel at the age of fifteen. Nine years later she died of tuberculosis, having been sanctified by the "little way of spiritual childhood." There is nothing infantile about this way. It is that of the beatitudes, manifesting the effect of God's love at work on human insufficiency.

Thomas (1st century) *July 3*

The Aramaic name Thomas means "twin," thus explaining John's calling the apostle by the Greek name "Didymus" (Jn 11:16; 20:24). While the synoptics are content to mention Thomas in the list of apostles (Mt 10:3; Ac 1:13), John, whose gospel is concerned with the various ways of "knowing" Jesus, seems to attach high importance to his reactions throughout. He makes Thomas in a way symbolic of the apostles' incredulity. Thomas sees the difficulties and dangers of a journey to Jerusalem, but fails to see its deeper meaning (Jn 11:16). His realism keeps him from displaying enthusiasm during the Supper discourse (Jn 14:1-6). After the resurrection he requires a visual and "carnal" knowledge of Christ instead of a "spiritual" faith (Jn 20:24-29). A few days afterwards we find him among the disciples who "know not" the Risen Christ (Jn 21:1-8). We know nothing of his career after Pentecost. Some traditions have him traverse beyond the frontiers of the Roman Empire to Persia and India. Such medieval concepts however, which allot a geographical region to each apostle, are based on legend only.

Thomas Aquinas (1225?-1274) *January 28*

Born near Monte Cassino in Italy, Thomas entered the Dominican order and became first a student, then a professor of theology at Paris. During the great period of the thirteenth century, he is the mouthpiece of Catholic thought. He achieved the first synthesis between the pagan philosophy of Aristotle and scriptural and Augustinian theology. With good reason his writings became the basis of priestly formation for several centuries. His learning was due to his exceptional intelligence, but also to his pronounced leaning towards prayer and contemplation.

Thomas Beckett (1117-1170) *December 29*

Totally devoted to the interests of the English crown, Thomas gave evidence of exceptional talent. When Henry II ascended the throne in 1154 he named him chancellor. When however seven years later he had him elected archbishop of Canterbury, Thomas became henceforward an exemplary servant of the Church and firmly rejected all lay interference. He was arrested but succeeded in reaching France, where he took refuge in the Abbey of Pontigny and lived a strictly monastic life for six years. Henry finally recalled him to his see, but Thomas continued to be as intransigent as ever. His enemies sought his head and he was assassinated in his cathedral.

Thomas More (1478-1535) *June 22*

Having acted as a professor of law, Thomas played a very important part in the public affairs of the English kingdom. He was chancellor to Henry VIII when the latter wanted to marry Anne Boleyn. When the king encountered Roman opposition and decided to withdraw the English Church from Roman authority, Thomas chose to relinquish his office. This cost him his life.

Timothy (1st century) *January 26*

Born at Lystra in Turkey (Ac 16:1) Timothy doubtless owed his knowledge of Scripture to his Jewish mother (2 Tm 3:15; 1:6), but his early education was chiefly Greek. When Paul passed through Lystra the second time he was already Christian. Paul had him circumcised in order not to scandalize the weak (Ac 16:1-3) and took him on his apostolic journeys (Ph 2:19-21; 1 Th 3:1-8; 1 Co 4:17; 16:10). According to tradition, Timothy died a martyr at Ephesus where Paul had left him at the head of the Church (1 Tm 1:3). The portrait which Paul has left us of Timothy is that of a timid man of great sensitivity who shows fidelity throughout all trials.

Titus (1st century) *January 26*

Titus was probably converted by Paul at Antioch where he had been born of Greek parents (Ac 15:2). He was affected by the misgivings which divided Christians of Jewish origin from those of Gentile. He refused to be circumcised (Ga 2:1-5). His keen conviction about Christian liberty where the ancient observances were concerned made him a suitable preacher for the Corinthians, who had suffered because of this (2 Co 8:6, 16; 12:18). Subsequently Paul entrusted him with the organization of the Church at Crete, where he lived doubtless until the end.

Turribius of Mongrovejo (1538-1606) *March 23*

Born at Mongrovejo (Spain), Turribius was named archbishop of Lima (Peru) at the age of forty-two under the reign of Philip II. He was struck by the material and spiritual misery of the Indians. He gave himself resolutely to the task of serving them, firmly opposing successive governors of Peru and the exactions of the Spanish colonists. He died ill and exhausted at the age of seventy.

Vincent (3rd century) *January 22*

A deacon of Saragosse in Spain, Vincent was martyred at Valence. He is for the Church of Gaul what Stephen was for Jerusalem, and Lawrence for Rome.

Vincent de Paul (1581-1660) *September 27*

"Monsieur Vincent" was parish priest of Clichy, chaplain to prisoners and director of several enterprises in Paris. His titles to renown are two: concern for the rural population for whom he designed the Lazarist congregation, and for the proletariat in the cities among whom the Sisters of Charity labored.

Vincent Ferrer (1350?-1419) *April 5*

This Spanish Dominican was totally dedicated to missionary preaching throughout the whole West. His vigorous style produced all the more conversions as he preached that the end of the world was near. He died during a missionary enterprise in Brittany.

Wenceslaus (903/05-929/35) *September 28*

During his four years of power, Wenceslaus, Duke of Bohemia, followed a pro-Western policy that alienated him from Byzantine influence. He sent the missionaries from the East home and invited in Bavarian clergy, thus placing his territory under the religious and political influence of Rome. It was this change of policy, coupled with a resurgence of paganism, that brought about his assassination.

FOURTH PART

General Indexes to the Guides

I. INDEX OF SCRIPTURE READINGS

Mark

John

Acts

II. INDEX OF THEMES

(Capital letters and boldface numbers indicate doctrinal discussions.)